T0333642

THE
WAY
THROUGH
THE
WOODS

THE
WAY
THROUGH
THE
WOODS

The green witch's guide to navigating life's ups and downs

REBECCA BEATTIE

Elliott&Thompson

First published 2024 by
Elliott and Thompson Limited
2 John Street
London WC1N 2ES
www.eandtbooks.com

ISBN: 978-1-78396-784-1

Copyright © Rebecca Beattie 2024

The Author has asserted her rights under the Copyright, Designs and Patents Act, 1988, to be identified as Author of this Work.

All rights reserved. No part of this publication may be reproduced, stored in or introduced into a retrieval system, or transmitted, in any form, or by any means (electronic, mechanical, photocopying, recording or otherwise) without the prior written permission of the publisher. Any person who does any unauthorized act in relation to this publication may be liable to criminal prosecution and civil claims for damages.

9 8 7 6 5 4 3 2 1

A catalogue record for this book is available from
the British Library.

Typesetting: Marie Doherty
Printed by CPI Group (UK) Ltd, Croydon, CR0 4YY

This book is dedicated to those carers of this world –
those who look out for the vulnerable, the broken and the
traumatised. The work you do can sometimes feel thankless
and undervalued, but I would like to assure you that you
do make a difference, and change is entirely possible.

CONTENTS

INTRODUCTION: LIFE'S CHALLENGES SENT TO TEST YOU

There was once a road through the woods
Before they planted the trees.
It is underneath the coppice and heath,
And the thin anemones.
Only the keeper sees
That, where the ring-dove broods,
And the badgers roll at ease,
There was once a road through the woods . . .

Rudyard Kipling

Night is falling. You have stayed out much later than you intended, and everybody knows you should never walk through the woods in the dark, but you are partway through now and to go back wouldn't make any sense. You wish your coat was a protection against more than just the cold and damp. Something is shuffling on the path ahead – is it a badger, making its way home to its sett? Or is it something more sinister? Concentrating on your breathing, you try to quicken your steps: in the dim light it would be easy to stumble and fall, and you must keep your footing. Thoughts are becoming muddled with anxiety, and it is hard to think logically about the direction you should go in. As your panic threatens to rise and engulf you, you will your body to cooperate. At this moment in time, you are in danger of completely losing sight not only of where the path is but of where you were going in the first place.

Folk tales are full of warnings about the dangers of the woods. Even the post-modern retellings of these stories echo the same advice: 'Never stray from the path through the forest,' writes Angela Carter in *The Company of Wolves*, and even in childhood the fairy tales talk of little else. Little Red Riding Hood warns us of wolves that run through the trees in the night, while Hansel and Gretel whisper of witches who dwell in the woods and eat little children. But what does the fairy tale have to do with real life?

When faced with the wonder of a woodland glade, is it any wonder that we feel inspired to wind our storytelling around the boles of the trees, draping them, moss-like, from the great limbs that rise above us? Of course, all these stories hint at the woodland as a metaphor for our inner landscape. Humans have always had one eye on the woodland as a place of wildness, representing something of our own psyches: our generation today is not the first to conclude that woodland spaces are magical and essential to our mental wellbeing. While woodland can be a place to walk, to sit and rest your back against a trunk, or to watch the signs of nature unfurling across the year, it can also be somewhere to take your troubles. When you are in the company of a being that has existed for centuries, it can sometimes help to put your own problems into perspective.

But what about those bigger issues – the ones you didn't ask for? We've all had them – the dramatic life changes that leave us sitting on our metaphorical backsides on the ground, wondering what hit us. It might be the sudden and unexpected end of a relationship, or the death of a loved one, or – even weirder as we expect it to be all plain sailing – the beginning of something positive in your life such as a new job, or a new relationship. These situations can all come with a sense of bewilderment, as you must gather in your wits and try to work out what just happened. You might also start to lose sight of yourself and forget who you were before.

That is what this book is about. How to navigate those sometimes-earth-shattering life changes that leave you feeling vulnerable, alone and afraid, those times when you think somehow that everyone except you knows what they are doing, that maybe you missed a turn on your way through the woods, or lost the map, and now you are stuck in an unfamiliar landscape, wondering how to get home. But before we get on to the business of those changes themselves, let's think about some of the tools we might need on this journey; if I am going to be your guide, I probably need to tell you why I can help you navigate this stretch of the journey.

Before we start, I'm not going to tell you that I'm the world expert on everything. In fact, I might go so far as to say I am quite ordinary. I don't believe in people setting themselves up as 'special', as it can lean into elitism. In fact, as I get older, I have come to realise we are all extraordinary beings. I am what is called a Gardnerian Wiccan. If that term is new to you (outside of *Charmed* or other fictional realms), for the purposes of this introduction, it's useful to know that Wicca is a spiritual path which is matriarchal in nature and seeks a spiritual connection with the divine in nature. It holds the divine feminine, in the form of the triple goddess – a concept we'll come back to later in the book – at its very heart. The only demons we battle are our own inner ones. For me nature is everything – a connection to the divine, a consoler when I am down, an inspiration when I need to create and sometimes just a comfort blanket to wrap myself in when the world feels a bit mean.

Wicca is a path that encourages study, and because I am naturally curious, over the years I've explored everything from psychology to neuro-linguistic programming (NLP) and hypnosis, to English literature and world religions. I've spent most of my adult life learning one subject after another – it's become a life choice of sorts – so I do have several tools in my basket to help me navigate the stony path through the woods, not least those we use as modern-day witches. As well as a closeness to nature, these include an understanding of the value of ritual and time being set aside for spiritual practice; knowing there is still magic in the world; an ongoing cooperative relationship with the divine; and an ability to sense where the road ahead may be leading. In this book, I want to share some of those tools with you – crafting exercises to get you in touch with your sense of inner playfulness and creativity, and rituals to help you punctuate your life changes with a little celebration to acknowledge them and give yourself some closure.

If you have not encountered ideas around magic or used the tarot before, it might feel a little odd at first, so I will tell you what I often say to my students: it is healthy to give yourself permission to believe in magic. But what is magic? This is a tricky concept, as there are many different definitions out there. However, rather than see it as a dark art belonging to the occult, I think of it as something more akin to creativity. When I do magic, it's a little like an active prayer – asking the universe to help me create a desired outcome under grace, as long as that does not involve harming others in the process. Just because you have asked for a change, however, that's not to say you will always get it. Magic can only really work if the thing you are asking for is capable of becoming that thing – you can't go against nature. For example, if I do a spell to turn someone into a donkey (think Bottom in *A Midsummer Night's Dream*), it is unlikely to happen, but if I ask for help in completing a project I am working on – a new home, a new relationship – and I am already working towards that goal, it is more likely to happen. Meanwhile, as I will explain further later, in consulting tarot cards, I am not necessarily divining the future or consulting an external force, I am simply exploring my own unconscious. I am using the cards, rather like a storytelling device, to identify what is around me and within me, but which I may not be consciously aware of – yet. If you feel sceptical right now, don't worry. I am one of the most cautious people I know, but over the years I have I have realised that life without enchantment would be a grey and colourless place. I prefer to live in a world where magic (creativity) and divination (storytelling) are a possibility rather than one of scientific certainty, where the goalposts often change as a new school of science disproves or opens up the theories of the one that came before.

I'm also a lifelong journal keeper. Feelings can be slippery things, like minnows, darting about and changing direction in the stream of life, and memory can fail us. In common with most people, I need time to process how I am feeling about something before I can articulate it to anyone else. Capturing the likeness of feelings on paper can be a helpful way of absorbing or analysing a particular situation, and acknowledging those emotions. Whatever you record, whether it's a lot or a little, it can be useful when looking back and assessing how things are (or were) for you. How you record your journaling – on paper, on voice memo, on film or in interpretive dance – is entirely up to you.

The point of life for me is that we're here, having a very physical experience. Wicca is an embodied religion, which means we're not in the business of hankering after heaven. For us, where we are now is where it's at – paradise is already on earth, and it's generally found in nature. That doesn't mean we don't believe in an afterlife, but Wiccans try to live life to the full, and we acknowledge that life can be challenging. Although the two things may be unconnected, my life as a priestess has corresponded with life being a twisty-turny thing that surprises me at every junction. Just when I think I know what I'm doing, circumstance jumps out from behind a tree and yells, 'Ha! Fooled you!'

In the twenty-five years or so since I began my path into paganism, I've experienced the end of several significant relationships (and therefore the beginning of others), the death of a very significant loved one, the realisation I was not going to have children, several career changes. I have also re-rooted my life from one geographical area to another (several times) and finally landed back where I began life – in rural Devon. And then there was the ending of my marriage (after a decade). In between then and now – and thank goodness – I spent a significantly sensible period in counselling, with a good therapist, who, for the sake of discretion, I will refer to as Shirley. That last one was a game changer. I would even go as far as to say that it saved my life. Now, whenever I am uncertain as to what to do, I think to myself, 'What would Shirley say?'

It's important that I give you a caveat at this point. As a witch, I'm used to doing magic to help me to feel empowered in any given situation (and I will tell you more about that later too). Magic, however, does not take away the need to act in the physical world, and it's not a cure-all. If you are undergoing one of the dramatic life changes that we are going to visit in this book, there are no short cuts; if you are someone who would benefit from the help of a properly trained and qualified professional, then I would urge you to get support that way. Similarly, if you are battling with any life-changing illnesses or health conditions while going through these changes, it's important you continue with your medical treatment. If you are neuro-divergent, and have found medication to be helpful, don't stop taking it. This book is really an extra tool on top of the ones you already have – it's not a substitute. But if, like me, you have a fiercely stubborn and independent streak, and you also want to take some real-life changes of your own, this book is here as a guide.

The Way Through the Woods echoes the theme of nature's seasonal cycles. I have grouped the life changes we'll be working with according to the season with which they chime. I have also made reference to the relevant magical foundations we will be working with during each of life's ups and downs – the appropriate planetary body that rules these particular changes or times in life, as well as the element: Earth, Air, Fire and Water. Similarly, I have given you the cardinal compass point you might be facing if you were in a witches' circle at this time, and the tarot card that you may discover if you consult the cards, to help you identify what to look out for. All of these details are contextual, and you can simply plant them in the back of your mind while you concentrate on the work at hand – navigating the changes in your life. We'll begin with winter, the hardest season of all. Winter is always a challenge – our death rates increase, along with our sickness rates, and our depression levels too. This means we will be looking at some of the 'bad boy' topics, including death and grieving – as well as endings in general – first. Yet out of these endings will come new beginnings, and from there we will move on to spring, to look at new relationships and family dynamics; summer will bring us to choosing to relocate and finding our flow. Finally, autumn will take us on a little tour around self-actualisation – reaching our fullest potential with the coming of age and the menopause.

Now, onto our first season, winter. Just as the pagan Wheel of the Year begins with midwinter in my model of the world, so winter is our starting place here too. It's the time of year when you get to see the bare bones of the world that are usually hidden beneath layers of foliage. As I wrote in my nature diary several years ago:

> Today the sun throws long shadows across the pathways that are paved with dead oak leaves and the grass still shows signs of heavy frost in spite of this late hour. Just standing to write this makes my toes feel the cold, but I am able to see pathways I haven't seen before because the trees and the undergrowth are so bare.

So, let's venture into the forest in winter as we begin our journey through the landscape of our lives and discover our way through the woods.

PART ONE
WINTER IN THE WOODS

There's a certain Slant of light,
Winter Afternoons . . .
When it comes, the Landscape listens –
Shadows – hold their breath –
When it goes, 'tis like the Distance
On the look of Death –

Emily Dickinson

THEMES: Changes that you haven't asked for but have come regardless, the illusion of control being revealed as false, legacy, abandonment, endings
PLANET: Saturn
ELEMENT: Earth
DIRECTION: North
TIME OF DAY: Night

In woodland, life goes inwards in winter. It stays small and quiet, waiting for the spring to come again and release it from the tight grip of the frost. And yet, when life has caused me to question everything, to mourn afresh old wounds that should have healed by now, it is to the woods that I come and bring my sorrows. Deep in the heart of my local temperate rainforest, I visit a pool in the river when I need to wash away my sadness. It is particularly nurturing first thing in the morning, before the woods have fully thrown off night, or last thing in the evening, just at the gloaming, when everyone else has gone home. I call it Witches' Spa – a twin waterfall carves a natural pool out of the bedrock, and a corresponding waterfall at the down-river end gives the impression of an infinity pool. After the rains, the water levels rise to their highest point and take on the hue of a cold Guinness, made peaty by the off-run of the moor. Leaves still circle and rise from the depths in the dead of winter, their brown shapes dancing and weaving in the fast current. When the river is in spate and I cannot make it all the way in, instead I hold on to an exposed curve of tree root to keep me steady.

When the sun shines on this pool, as it does only in the fading light of the afternoon, the water becomes crystal clear, lucid and turquoise in its intensity. Sitting a while on its banks, I can feel the limpid depths reflecting my mood, allowing clear sight and thoughts to flow like the water itself. If ever I need to get in touch with my own inner self and the wisdom locked away inside, I come here, notebook in hand. Here, at least, there is comfort and solace. Here there is a soothing gentleness to winter in the woods that can help us to navigate the hardest parts of human existence.

CHAPTER ONE

THE JOURNEY THROUGH DEATH AND . . .

You would know the secret of death.
But how shall you find it unless you
seek it in the heart of life?

Kahlil Gibran

TAROT CARDS: Death and the Six of Swords

In 2005, I lost my mother to cancer. I was thirty; she was sixty-one. The illness crept up on us and took hold very quickly. The cancer was an aggressive kind. She started to feel unwell in November, then died on New Year's Day.

Looking back on that time now, almost twenty years on, the experience can still land a punch straight to my gut that leaves me winded and gasping for breath. I remember fragments – the phone call when she told me she would be dying soon, which left me howling on the floor; the visits to the hospital in search of hopeless healing; the conversation my dad, my sister and I had on a walk to our favourite spot on the moors, when I said I wanted to be with her at her passing. I consider myself deeply privileged to have been with Mum at the moment of her dying, to have 'midwifed' that transition and to have come so close to death. It was a deeply transformative and spiritual experience.

There was a day in the hospital when I was alone with Mum. The elderly lady in the next bed was hidden behind a closed curtain. I was sitting on Mum's bed and she and I were talking about faith and religion. At this point I was just starting to explore Wicca. Mum was telling me that she had experienced moments of prayer that left her feeling comforted, supported by an unseen presence, and I was agreeing with her. Just at that moment we realised something had happened in the neighbouring bed. The lady's daughter let out a cry and, as she did, I closed my eyes and 'felt' the lady leaving. A feeling of her continued presence, accompanied by a warm and strong impression of her being all right now, washed over me.

Mum saw what was happening, and let me experience it for a few moments. Then she whispered to me, 'Did you feel that?' and I nodded. Somewhere in those moments, we both took comfort from the fact that I had felt the presence of the elderly lady after she had died. Of course, that is a matter of faith, and can never be proved, but it gave us a moment of hope in an otherwise hopeless situation.

Death is a difficult thing to write about, and even harder to talk about. Even now I am choosing my words incredibly carefully. We tend to talk in metaphors when death comes into the conversation – we talk about someone's 'passing', their 'transition', and for those left behind we say, 'I am so sorry for your loss', as if they have mislaid a pair of gloves or their house keys. In fact, I would go one step further and say our society has done everything it can to divorce us from death – it becomes something that happens in private, behind closed doors, rarely spoken about openly. Even if you haven't yet encountered the death of someone significant yet, death and grief are an inevitable part of life. You may find this chapter helpful to read so that you can better understand those around you who are in mourning, as it is a blessing to be able to respond to them with openness and kindness, rather than to shy away for fear of saying something inadvertently hurtful.

If, like me, you spend time in nature, you will have seen the traces – the feathers left behind on the woodland path after a night-time's hunting, the bones of a once-pony on the moor, or strands of wool left attached to the heather. As a child I even took home the skull of a sheep – its chalk-white, hard lines revealing the scaffolding that lay beneath the face, yet somehow not attached to the concept of the living being that once wore that face.

The truth is, modern paganism, like its ancient predecessors, wasn't all that helpful in providing me with a manual for grief when I lost my mother. To our ancestors, death was all around; it was not the source of any mystery beyond what happens to our souls once we transition out of the physical existence. While Christianity is built with the death of someone significant at its core, the ancient pagan faiths focused all their efforts on trying to imagine what the afterlife would be like for the deceased person. For example, the Egyptian *Book of the Dead* contains detailed spells and rituals to prevent the dead person from being consumed by crocodiles, or to stop their head falling off (yes, really), but there is nothing there to help with grief – in fact one of the spells is to prevent the deceased person from being replaced in life, as if they ever could be. Similarly, the handbooks we have all come to rely on in the West – for example, the work of Elisabeth Kübler-Ross, who I will talk more about later – were originally written for the person who was grappling with a terminal diagnosis, and not their loved ones left behind. Kübler-Ross, later in her life, worked with the 'grieving expert' David Kessler, and adapted the stages of grief to fit many other situations. Yet the truth is, like the pairing in tarot of the Death card and the Six of Swords (a journey across water), the deceased loved one is not the only person going on a voyage here. When you lose a loved one, your whole life changes too.

After my mum died, I felt I needed to know how other people had encountered death and how their lives were changed as a result.

I came to learn there is a strange beauty in it, how we shall all face our own death one day, as well as the death of everyone we have ever known and loved, and more besides. In this chapter, I will share some of the small beauties I discovered, as well as some of the terrors. It comes with one caveat, however. In the same way that moving through grief will never be a linear process, every person's experience of death is unique to them. What you discover will make your journey through this sometimes alien landscape your own. I offer these thoughts, then, to give you a sense of my own pathway through this dark time, which I hope will help illuminate your own.

PREPARATION FOR THE JOURNEY: BEFORE DEATH

If truth be told, nothing can really prepare you for death. A sudden death can leave people reeling – with unfinished business, words of love unspoken, arguments unresolved. If you are given warning of the event, you may enter a stage called 'anticipated grief'. In my case, I lay awake each night thinking of my mother and what was likely to happen in the coming weeks, shaking at the thought of what we would face. My limbs would feel cold and my teeth would chatter. I almost became accustomed to the intense heavy weight in my chest, to the way my breath would catch in my throat and my heart would stop momentarily each day. In my own naive way, I held on to my one mantra, 'Please let her go quickly and not suffer for too long.'

Yet I was lucky in that I had several people who had been through this process ahead of me and were able to share their experiences. This meant I was able to be there for my mum, to be part of the tag-team with the rest of the family, each in turn cooking, cleaning, going with her to appointments. Whatever else was going on, she had us with her, as the rest of life was put on hold, and yet, for the person dying, this process can be a profoundly isolating experience. People can sometimes talk about the person as if they are not there any more, as if their opinion doesn't matter. If you are present with someone in the end stages of life, it is important you don't do this. Just ask them what they need, what they want and do your best to fulfil their requests. You might be called on to advocate on their behalf. Don't worry that you might make mistakes and get things wrong – the important thing is that you are present.

TRY THIS: A WOODLAND SENSORY WALK

Time in nature can offer us valuable moments of solace and solitude when the busyness of death takes over, and I would encourage you to take advantage of what is on offer near you. It might be a garden, a park or a woodland path. Walking through the woods in winter is a full sensory experience. Because the trees are stripped back to their cold branches, without the softening of the green covering of leaves, a wood can seem bare, harsh and very cold. But if you wrap up against the inclement wind, or the unexpected showers of rain or snow, you can start to discover a world that you never knew existed when the woods were haloed in green.

In my local wood, the first thing that comes alive is my sense of smell. The loamy scent of the earth becomes pungent; each footfall releases wafts of it. It smells like the taste of root vegetables – of beetroot and potato with the soil barely dusted free. It smells like vetivert and violet leaf – green, brown and heavy with a musk of its own.

The second sense to come alive is my hearing. In winter, the birds are subdued and still, with only the most resolute of souls singing in the depths between the trees. The occasional trill of a blackbird's voice, clear as glass. The throaty cawing of crows, indignant that I have disturbed their peace with my clumsy trampling of bare twigs and broken leaves, dry, brittle and tense. The third sense is sight – what wonders we can discover among the abandoned trees of deepest winter, when only the bare bones of the forest are visible, and only the most determined of walkers make their way here.

I would love it if you could take yourself to your nearest woodland in winter and start to use your five senses in noticing what is around you. If you are a city dweller, and finding a woodland is impossible, then you can visit a city park instead and gain just as much insight as they are usually filled with trees. Perhaps find a tree that particularly appeals to you. What can you see, hear, smell, taste and feel? Using your senses in nature in this way not only helps to familiarise you with the world around you, but this 'mindful' approach to observing it can help to bring you out of grief, anticipated or otherwise, and gently lead you back into the now. When the future seems bleak, and the past is full of hurt, sometimes the now is the most nurturing place to be.

EMBARKING ON THE SHADES OF THE DEAD, OR THE MOMENT OF DEATH ITSELF

For my mother, the moment of death was peaceful. Obviously, this is not always the case. Each person's experience is different and, again, you must be guided by the person themselves, as well as your own beliefs.

Your loved one might go through several different states of consciousness in the process of dying. My mum had entered a state of altered consciousness in the last few days. As the end drew closer, she spent less time awake and present. As I wrote in my grief journal at the time:

Mum sleeps on, her breathing peaceful at last, her face clear of the pain and distress she felt when she was awake and still with us. I stroke her hair while Dad dozes in the chair on the other side of the bed.

Outside the day breaks on a cold January morning in Devon. The trees are bare, and a cold wind blows off the high moors and into this wide valley. The window is open just a crack because she always wants to have just a little bit of fresh air. The heavy net curtain blows in the current. Somewhere a tractor starts up and I hear voices hushed in the corridor outside. Mum stirs:

'It is so peaceful here,' she whispers, almost under her breath, and then drifts away again.

I lay my head on her pillow, place my mouth next to her ear and start to speak gently to her.

I am not sure I could tell you exactly what I said to my mum. I remember words of reassurance, words of love. I do recall assuring her that it was OK to leave us, that we were releasing her. My feeling at the time was that her experience was so difficult, I did not want her worrying about us, though somehow she always knew it would come to this.

'I will never make old bones,' she would say to me with a wry smile. But that was when her death was some vague and far-off future event. When it came to it, she knew long before the doctors the path she'd be taking, though she shielded us from it. Always so quick to protect everyone else, the last person she would look after was herself.

In time, her hospital room became a cocoon for us, away from the rest of the world, where we were encased in a shell that at any moment might crack and send us all sprawling. If you are walking this path with a loved one, it is important for you to be able to sequester yourself away with them and just focus on what they need, even if you are only able to do this one moment at a time in between the rest of life's demands. Later, this will be an important landmark as you navigate the rest of the woods, knowing that you took those moments and cherished them while you could.

The actual moment of Mum's death was one of the most profoundly spiritual experiences I have had in this lifetime. I felt her passing, just as I had felt the lady in the hospital depart previously. Ever since then, I have been sure I can sense the departed person at funerals. Is it their soul that comes back to visit? I always like to think we get to see our own funeral and who has turned up. It might be delusional, it might be weird, but it gives me immense comfort to feel that the person I am mourning is there and present.

TRY THIS: CREATING YOUR OWN GRIEF ARCHETYPES

You will find throughout this chapter that I talk about death as if it is a real person. Facing moments of devastation head on, writers the world over have been employing this technique for centuries. With figures such as the Ghost of Christmas Yet to Come in Dickens' *A Christmas Carol*, and Death in Terry Pratchett's *Mort*, it becomes a way of removing the fear of death, while at the same time humanising it. Humans throughout history have created archetypes – figures who enable us to explain the unexplainable and make it more palatable.

It could be argued that we have distanced ourselves from these archetypes over time, just as we have divorced ourselves from the process of death and dying, and it can be beneficial to think about how you might meet and greet your own death archetypes. Writing your own story or creating a narrative in response to your own experiences is a deeply empowering and nourishing way to approach the process of change. It can help you to sift through events, make sense of your experiences and acknowledge your emotional responses to them, which are so important. Later, sharing these can be healing for other people also.

Perhaps like the ancient Greeks you might imagine being carried, Six of Swords-like, in a boat over the river Styx to the realm of the dead, after paying a coin to Charon the ferryman to cover the fare. How would you feel during the crossing? Or perhaps you might encounter an ageless figure like the goddess Hecate at the crossroads in the woods, as she holds aloft a lantern to illuminate the way, throwing light into the shadows between the trees.

You might find it healing at this point to consider what your own archetype would look like. How would it appear to you, and in what setting? How would it usher you in? As an example, I have created my own example of a death archetype.

Once upon a time, in a land not so very far away, they lived an imperfect goddess called Elizabeth. She was a gentle soul, who liked to fill her days with books and nature and dreaming. One day, when the last of the leaves had finally fallen from the trees in the winter gales, and the trees swayed in the cold north wind, Elizabeth decided to set out on a quest – to go in search of her lost mother and discover the mysteries of life and death. She packed a bag of food for her and her little dog, she placed her favourite necklace around her neck, and her bracelets on her wrists. Closing the door behind her, she set one foot on the path. As she walked, the wind brought whispers of snow and ice, but Elizabeth was undeterred. She was resolute: she must learn what she could in the woods.

Along the trail, the imperfect goddess reached a tunnel carved into the hillside. She peered inside. She could see a faint glow of green light at the other end, so she pressed on.

As Elizabeth emerged from the tunnel, she knew that she was now in a different part of the woods – much further in than the distance she'd walked. She noticed the quiet descending around her. She had often heard her mother say that this was the realm where the crone lived, her black cloak sheltering her head, her pack of dogs around her, with the lantern she held aloft to light the way. The imperfect goddess knew she must seek out the crone if she was to learn the secret of death.

It was then that she noticed a side gate leading into the deepest part of the woods. The path underfoot was covered over in dead leaves and fallen twigs. Each step she took was accompanied by the sounds of crackling and rustling. Coming around the next bend in the path, she saw the crone up ahead, and her little dog ran towards her. The crone was entranced by the little dog and the way it wrapped itself around her ankles in joy. If this was how the little dog responded, thought Elizabeth, then the crone could not possibly be someone to fear.

Our ability to tell stories can illuminate our path through these winter woods of grief following the death of a loved one, and lay a trail for those around us who are also taking this journey. I would encourage you to keep your notebook handy, and trace your own story as you go. You can follow the story of Elizabeth as we continue across this chapter and beyond through the different phases of grief and loss and into each new season.

NAVIGATION: GRIEF AND GRIEVING

'Good day to you, ma'am,' began Elizabeth, her voice sounding shriller than she intended.

'I am not the Queen,' replied the crone. 'You may call me Margaret.'

'Margaret,' stammered Elizabeth. 'I wonder if you might help me. I come here in search of the secrets of death,' she said. 'I want to find the place where death lives.'

Margaret nodded and looked thoughtful.

'Are you sure you are ready to learn such mysteries while you are still so young?'

The imperfect goddess thought for a moment but, remembering her mother's warm embrace, she nodded.

People talk about grief as if it is a vast dark forest to push through, but I would like to propose a different model. It's not a place you go, but a companion who meets you in the woods and stays with you on your onward journey. It is important to find ways, such as in the previous exercise, to enable us to befriend grief, so that we do not try to resist it. To refuse this process would be to push the feelings down and not process them properly: this later can lead to illness, both physical and mental. It is important to acknowledge your thoughts and fears as they arise, and to remember that while you are vulnerable right now, you won't always be so. For some people, grief is an unpredictable creature, as my close friend and fellow priestess Alatarial shared with me: 'Grief is a wild beast,' she said. 'It raises its head in ways we never thought of – impacting on all aspects of our life.' Grief can sometimes sneak up on you and pull your pigtails, but it can also give you a hard smack round the chops that leaves your face stinging and your tears flowing. Sometimes, you are left breathless and wondering if you will survive it. But in time you get used to its presence in your life; while grief doesn't ever go away, you can learn to live with it in companionable silence. Make a place for grief at your table and share a meal together, or write grief a letter telling him or her how they have made you feel, and also how they have helped you in this journey.

While no one can predict how you will feel, there are some useful 'roadmaps' you can consult for the journey you are on, to help you identify those cleverly concealed grief pangs. At this point I am going to reintroduce you to Elisabeth Kübler-Ross, a Swiss psychologist who spent most of her early working life with patients who were terminally ill. She observed that people would go through five identifiable stages when they were coming to terms with their own death: denial, anger, bargaining, depression and acceptance, but these just as easily apply to the bereaved also.

Kübler-Ross's theory has been debunked or discredited in some quarters, but this is usually because people misunderstand how the five stages of grief work. The word 'stages' suggests something that will run consecutively, but Kübler-Ross herself stated quite clearly that the stages are not linear – not everyone will experience all five of them, and you may find you loop back round and experience some of them more than once. Do remember – the map is not the territory. A model is there as a guideline, but life can look and feel very different from the landscape that is drawn on paper.

So, let's see what these stages look like in real life.

DENIAL

Our grief companion begins by bringing us denial. This does not necessarily mean that you deny that the loss has happened – you might feel disbelief when you are still in a state of shock. If what you have experienced is a death, or the ending of a significant relationship, this is the part where you might wake up each morning and, for the first few seconds of conscious awareness, wonder if it was all a bad dream and if your loved one will emerge, Bobby Ewing-style, from the shower. At this point you might be clinging to what Kübler-Ross and Kessler refer to as the 'safe world' – the old reality that has now passed, as opposed to the new one you have not yet got your head around. Go gently on yourself. The sense of denial will dissipate, but you need to give yourself time.

ANGER

Anger often happens when the full extent of the loss you have experienced starts to sink in: you may feel angry at the rest of the world for not being fully aware of what has just happened, or at the lost loved one for going, or with yourself for something you did or didn't do. The thing to bear in mind here is that your emotions are not logical, linear things that always have a root cause. You might feel angry for no good reason at all. You can see this in my own grief diaries, true to Kübler-Ross's model:

> 17 January 2005
> I am back home and due to start my first day back at work. I feel scratchy, tempestuous, Little Miss Firecracker, almost willing people to say something clumsy and ill-timed so that I can unleash it a little and whip them sharply around the face with my words. Of course, that would be unfair, so I will it to nestle down inside my belly, coiling around on itself, hissing its forked tongue as it dozes in a light sleep, with one eye open.

Many years on, I am learning how poor we are (collectively) at managing anger as an emotion – both our own and other people's. You could say that women in Western society are trained not to 'do' anger, as it tends to make people uncomfortable, but this affects men as well. Men are taught to channel it (and other difficult emotions) through 'manly pursuits' such as sports or competitive activities that are designed to vent their inner warrior, while women seethe silently into whatever they are doing to distract themselves. When we don't know what to do with a particular emotional response, we often go into avoidance – side-stepping the emotion, or evading the angry person, and hoping it will go away.

I would invite you, if you are feeling that hot, writhing anger, to seek ways of expressing it or expelling the energy it creates. Journal it, sing it, paint it or express it through whatever physical activity you favour – walking, swimming, running – or scream it into a pillow, shout it to the hills. Think about what works best for you. If you don't, it will turn in on you, and you can damage your health (both physical and mental) if you don't vent that pressure cooker. And it's not just your health that suffers, it's the unfortunate person who asks the wrong question at the wrong time and gets hit in the chest with both barrels.

BARGAINING

The third stage the grief companion brings, according to Kübler-Ross and Kessler, is bargaining. This doesn't mean you are off to the market to haggle; it means you start 'should-ing'. My best friend Lizzie always says to me, 'Stop should-ing all over yourself – it's a dirty habit', and this is what we mean by bargaining. We start to think about what we should have done better – what we got wrong, what we didn't think of until it was too late – and then we start bargaining with the universe: 'I should have told Mum I loved her more'; 'I should have gone home more quickly when I got the call'; 'If only I could take her place – my life for her own.'

DEPRESSION

Depression inevitably comes along to join you on your walk through the woods with grief at some point in the journey. Depression is the listless, low mood that comes when the reality of your situation starts to sink in. Just be aware, there is a difference between clinical depression – the long-lasting type that may or may not have a trauma-based reason for it, so may come and stay for a long period for no apparent reason – and the depression that comes with grief. It's up to you whether or not to seek medical intervention for grief-related depression – only you can decide if medication would help or not. I chose to write about grief instead, first in my journals and later in my creative writing, and then I worked it through with a counsellor too. In hindsight, if I had found the right counsellor earlier, I would have started that work sooner.

ACCEPTANCE

This is the stage of the journey when all the swirling emotions have stopped carrying you round and round in the tornado like Dorothy in *The Wizard of Oz*. It doesn't mean you are over the grief and completely on the mend as if nothing happened – you may continue to dip in and out of any one or a combination of the four other stages – but the reality of what you have experienced begins to seep into your bones.

However, one thing is for certain, having experienced a grief, you will never quite be the same person again. Something in the process changes us irrevocably. It's that change process again, isn't it?

CHARTING YOUR COURSE THROUGH MODERN RITES OF PASSAGE

With Margaret leading the way, Elizabeth made her way deeper into the woods. They had reached the deepest part of the wood, where the only sounds were their footsteps and the wind overhead. Then she began to hear the sound of running water. Up ahead, she could see a tall, slender heron standing in the water, its sad, grey plumage almost invisible against the colour of the river. Margaret turned to the imperfect goddess.

'Here is where I must leave you,' she said, 'but first you must take off all your finery, because these are earthly things and there is no place for them in the land of the dead.'

Elizabeth removed her red cloak and placed it down on the river-bank. Then she removed each of her bracelets and all her rings and finally her necklace, leaving them in the little pile on the cloak.

'Now you must take the silver path,' whispered Margaret. So the imperfect goddess Elizabeth sat down on the banks of the river and removed her sturdy boots. As she dipped her toes into the icy water, the cold felt like a thousand tiny knives cutting her feet. She realised she could not walk through the water in her long skirts, so she removed them. She turned to Margaret to look for reassurance, but Margaret had already walked away, leading the little dog back through the woods.

Funerals and other rites of passage form an important function in the grieving process. Rites of passage are those moments that allow us to acknowledge the importance of the person or phase of life that we've lost, and to let it go with love. Without the process of releasing, we can be left with unresolved feelings, which will often come back to haunt us.

Our ancient ancestors understood the value of ritual, but it is something we modern humans have become rather detached from. For millennia, humans have found ways of letting someone go at the end of their life. In the early 1990s, an ancient burial site was uncovered on a remote part of Dartmoor, on Whitehorse Hill. A burial cist (a stone box-shape placed in the earth) was found on the side of a hill where peat-cutting had been taking place. When it was excavated, archaeologists discovered it was the grave of a warrior – not a male but a female fighter, beautifully preserved by the peat soil. Whitehorse Hill Woman had been buried in the Early Bronze Age (between 1730 and 1600 BCE) with all manner of magical items to go with her on her journey into the afterlife. Her remains had been buried in a bear's pelt, along with 200 beads made of clay, shale, tin from local mines and amber beads that had come from the Baltic. This find has changed the way we are seeing our own history, as it proves that the people of the Early Bronze Age had complex beliefs about living and dying, which we are only just beginning to uncover. Similar stories crop up all over the world, as archaeologists find evidence of funeral rites that date back to the beginning of history.

Today, as we prepare to say goodbye to a loved one, we can take our inspiration from our ancient ancestors, creating our own rituals and making our own rites of passage more personal and relevant by considering what we would like our loved one to take with them. Even if you are tied to a more traditional funeral by your family or cultural circumstances, you could still hold your own private ceremony later, to include all the ritual elements that personalise the rite to you and your loved one. For example, if your family service must include religious music, but you know your loved one would appreciate non-religious music more, then you can include that in your later celebration of their life. Just as with Whitehorse Hill Woman, when we buried our mum, my siblings and I all placed gifts in the coffin with her – a significant crystal, a poem, a photograph.

If the funeral is for your loved one, there is also an expectation that you are hosting it and seeing to the needs of everybody there, and this is where emotional clumsiness can play out. My family decided to do my mother's funeral slightly differently. To allow ourselves some privacy, we held the burial itself before the funeral, and then went on to have a public service in the local church.

The day of the funeral dawned cold, dark and blustery. The rain was falling not only in droves, but sideways. The wind was whipping it up and under our brollies and wrapping it around our legs. The men who carried the coffin stood by the graveside with no umbrellas: the water was pouring down their faces and dripping off their noses and collars. I wanted to offer them a tissue or an umbrella, but knew that they were expected to endure it without complaint.

We all stood and wept as they lowered the lovely willow casket into the earth, not knowing the difference between nature's tears and our own. Then we went to the church service.

I remember the sense of the family being in a space that was formal, but public, of the official ceremony and wake that followed feeling much less open and more performative than the family burial. It can be hard to express how you're feeling at a funeral and the emotional insensitivities of others can sting. For this reason, I would encourage you to separate private from public, and create some sacred space for yourself later to help with this otherwise unexpressed grief.

Sophie, a yoga teacher and tarot reader from London, recently lost her dad, Alfred, very suddenly. Alfred had lived in Europe for many years, but he was Vietnamese by birth. While the family held a funeral at a natural burial ground in Surrey, Sophie also found some relief in exploring rituals from her dad's own tradition. In Vietnamese culture, it's important to mark the passing of a loved one for a particular period (either a hundred days or forty days, depending on the regional beliefs) following their death, as this is the length of time it takes for the soul of the deceased person to be reborn. As this is a culture that, like Wicca, venerates ancestors, offerings are also given to the departed loved one to ensure they are kept happy and benevolent. Sophie created an altar space at home to Alfred's memory and would start each day by lighting some incense to him and giving him gifts of food. She has found revisiting her dad's cultural rituals, particularly for death and grief, very reassuring and consoling.

TRY THIS: AN INCENSE TO SEND A MESSAGE OF LOVE

Across the world, and since the beginning of history, incense has played an important part in sacred ceremonies. In ancient Egypt, the use of frankincense in the temples was so common that a trade route opened to the land of Punt (somewhere in the region of modern-day Ethiopia) to ensure that the valuable resin could reach the sacred temples further north. If you have spent any time in a modern Catholic church, you'll be familiar with the scent. In a witches' circle, too, we create and burn sacred incenses before and during our rituals.

In the days following my mother's death, I found it helpful to go out into her garden and burn quantities of incense that I had made. I saw the smoke as a message of love, sent up through the air, hoping to reach her wherever she was.

To burn loose incense, you will need a roll of charcoal discs (available in international supermarkets or online) and a censer or thurible, as well as a pair of sugar or kitchen tongs. Don't worry – although you can buy specially made censers, you don't have to: what's important is that whatever you use is made of something that won't shatter if it gets hot. You can create your own censer using an old mug, which is quite handy, as the handle allows you to move it around safely.

Fill the censer up to about two centimetres below the brim with earth, sand or salt. That is to prevent the mug from getting too hot. You will place the charcoal disc on top of this when you have lit it. But first, let's make an incense . . .

You will need:

* A sprig of rosemary leaves, cut into small pieces, or half a teaspoon of dried rosemary
* A teaspoon of dried sage

* A teaspoon of frankincense resin (available online or at herbalists)
* A teaspoon of myrrh resin
* Six drops of patchouli essential oil

Begin by grinding the herbs in a pestle and mortar, then add the frankincense and myrrh resin, and finally the essential oil.

Light your charcoal disc by holding it in a pair of tongs and then over a candle flame or lit gas stove. The tongs are there to prevent you from burning your fingers. When the disc starts to spark, place it on top of the censer. Leave it until it has turned grey: it is then ready to use. Add a small pinch of the incense at a time – a little goes a long way. Also, it is a good idea to keep a window open for ventilation and keep your smalls – children, non-human animals and birds – away from the incense smoke.

At this point you might choose to say some words of love, or to read aloud your departed beloved's favourite poem or, if you are feeling brave, to sing their favourite song.

ARRIVING AND DISEMBARKING: THE NEXT STAGE AND HOW LONG WILL I GRIEVE?

Elizabeth took another step into the river, feeling the pull of the current and the sharp stones under her bare feet. She looked up ahead and saw the path ahead of her. Night was now falling. The moon was ranging overhead, hunting with her pack of hounds. Clouds drifted across the night sky, but the stars had not yet come out. One bright star alone hung in the sky – Sirius, the dog star. The waters of the river glowed silver in the night and, as the imperfect goddess walked onwards, she noticed there were no owls in this part of the wood. There was just the hollow sound of water rushing over stones, and the swish of her feet moving through the water. She could not tell how long she had been walking.

After a time, Elizabeth reached a glade where the trees stood back to create a rounded lawn. She stepped out of the water, feeling momentary relief as her numbed feet felt the gentle scratching of the short, stubby grass. She realised that she was opposite the entrance to a cave and standing outside was the tall, lonely figure of a man, his features obscured by a hood that was pulled down almost to his eyes.

'Hello,' she said tentatively. 'Is this the way to the land of the dead?'

The man nodded and stood to one side. He gestured with his hand, indicating that she should enter.

People often wonder how long they'll be grieving their loved one for. At this point, I could write any number of platitudes – how long is a piece of string; how long did you love them for when they were living, and many others besides. The truth is everybody is different. For some, the grieving process is perfunctory – they might appear to move on quite rapidly after the death; for others, it can last years. In my own experience, nearly twenty years on from the death of my mother, I still have occasions where it rises like a wellspring and I'm left howling again.

For the first year after I lost my mum, I have no memory of anything. It was as though I was so shrouded in grief I existed in a bubble and I wasn't really functioning in the world. I attended the same training course twice in that year, without realising I'd already done it once before. This state of existence can be difficult for the people around you, if they're not suffering in the same way. You can appear isolated from them, unreachable, and in many ways you are. No one else can experience the same grief as you, so it is very difficult for others to understand.

For me, those first few years were punctuated not only by the death of my mum, but by the ending of some significant relationships.

I had friends who disappeared, not quite knowing how to respond to me, and some of them never returned. I also found that I made some ill-judged decisions about my life. (Please see the remaining chapters for more evidence of this!) At these times, remembering what you are grateful for in your life can give you a positive tether to hold on to.

READING THE MAP: TRANSITIONING INTO YOUR NEW LIFE

The way forward was now within complete darkness. Elizabeth placed her hands against the cold, damp walls of the cave and inched her way ahead, one step at a time. She felt entombed, regretting bitterly that she'd made this attempt when she could have just stayed at home, safe and happy with her little dog.

Then somewhere in the darkness, a flare of light, as if a flint had been struck. Elizabeth saw by the lamplight the face of the crone, Margaret, once more.

'How did you come to be here?' asked the imperfect goddess. 'I thought you'd left me in the woods.'

'I am the light in the darkness,' said Margaret. 'I am she who is with you when all you feel is alone and cold and scared. You must face the god and ask him what you would seek. For he holds the secret to many things. Take my hand,' Margaret said, 'and we will journey on together.'

When I was initiated into Wicca in 2006, a year and a half after my mother's death, it represented an important rite of passage to me – the death of my old self and the birth of a new version of me, who had to learn to live without my mother. In nature, no death is considered 'wasteful'. A fallen tree in the woods soon becomes the birthplace of new growth – fungus, insect life, mulch for young trees. As I walk through my local wood, I am often struck by how quickly nature reclaims and repurposes each and every old tree or branch. In this way every death also marks a new beginning, and every new beginning marks the death of something that you are leaving behind.

During the early years of my Wiccan training, I couldn't have a tarot reading without the Death card popping up. Now, if you have ever watched the 1973 James Bond film *Live and Let Die* (and let's face it, who hasn't?), the chances are your first response at hearing about the tarot is either one of fear or one of derision, especially when it comes to the Death card. Even the deck used in the film (the Witches' Tarot) has developed a sinister reputation, often eliciting gasps from people who assume it is a bad thing. But it's not that simple. The tarot is an important record of human archetypes and can be a very helpful tool in uncovering what is happening around you but of which you might not be consciously aware. The Swiss psychologist Carl Jung (1875–1961) famously worked on his theory of archetypes because he had a great affinity with the tarot, but knew it was unlikely to get over its stigma and be accepted by mainstream psychologists. This important work then became the basis of many other psychological tools, like Abraham Maslow's 'Hierarchy of Needs', which we will look at in Chapter Eight.

Now, I might have been a little paranoid about the presence of Death every time I touched a tarot deck. However, if we think about this logically, I had just experienced the most devastating loss and I was undergoing a significant transition of my own. Not only was I experiencing my Saturn Return at the end of my twenties – a period of upheaval we'll touch upon later – but I was also transforming my adult life onto the path that would eventually lead me to the present day. It was a big deal.

The Death card, then, can signify death itself – it often depicts the skeletal figure of Death sitting astride a horse, crossing a battle-field that is littered with bodies, both the young and the old, the rich and the poor, all of whom are rendered equal by death. However, the card can also be interpreted as a transformation, such as an emotional, spiritual or psychological ending, and a new beginning: 'Death and . . .' For example, the death of the old you and the birth of a new version of yourself.

The figure of Death on a tarot card is not the only death archetype to embody a sense of 'Death and . . .', with something new coming into being in its aftermath or existing alongside it. Every culture has a figure who represents the dual processes of death and the resultant transformation it brings. Baron Samedi, one of the *lwa* or spirits of Haitian Vodou is depicted as a man with a top hat and cane, yet a human skull dances beneath. Similarly, the Norse goddess Hel is depicted with two halves to her face – one the beautiful countenance of a young woman, the second a bared skull. All these death archetypes represent, through their stories, several qualities. Sometimes they accompany the soul on its journey to the afterlife; sometimes they intercede on the person's behalf. Sometimes their role is to help with the process of redemption. If you have grown up or live in a Christian environment, this might be a familiar theme. Jesus is an archetype of death and resurrection, just like the ancient Greek Dionysus, and Wiccan visions of the male god. Such figures perform a crucial role in human society, since they humanise our own mortality and make the prospect of our own deaths slightly less intimidating. Jung posited that certain archetypes are present in the collective unconscious of all of humanity, so that, no matter which culture you look at, there will be similar stories and myths about similar gods and heroes (or heroines). While every spiritual path is slightly different, they also have a lot in common, and it's important to embrace your own belief system, unapologetically, whatever its teachings are on living and dying. If you are bereaved, it's this that will keep you and support you in the difficult months ahead.

MOVING ON: PLANNING FOR SIGNIFICANT DAYS

Margaret held aloft the lantern and led the way through the darkness. They continued onward and reached a cavernous room. Elizabeth could see a dais up ahead, with a tall-backed throne. Sitting on the throne was the tall man she had met at the entrance to the cave, but instead of a hood he now wore a headdress of fine antlers.

The imperfect goddess suddenly felt angry. Had this all been a trick? She stepped forward, meaning to speak in reverence, but instead her anger unleashed itself and slapped around his knees like a scourge.

'Why did you make me come all this way, when you were waiting for me there at the beginning?'

He smiled at her and she realised that, although she had thought he looked grim, his face was kindly and his voice, when he spoke, was gentle to her ear.

He said, 'I will be waiting for you at the end of life, just as I was there at the beginning. You must love and be loved, and you must lose that love to me. You must be willing to explore the darkest of woods and the sunniest of meadows. My embrace is the last you will feel, and yet it will be one full of warmth and love. For to learn the mysteries of life and death, you must risk everything. You must place your heart fully into everything you do, because without life, there cannot be death, and without death, there cannot be life. Is it your will to continue?' he asked, and she looked up into his gentle face and nodded. 'Then I can reveal to you the secrets of death and life and love.'

Once more, her anger flared.

'Why must you take everything that I love?' she asked, and he smiled once more.

'Because without love,' he said, 'there would be no life, and without death there would be no life, as no one can live forever, except in our hearts and in our memories. Nature will continue, whether you paint your flowers in the meadows or not, but it is enriched by your presence and enriched by the heart, and by your curiosity to learn the secrets of life and death.' He gestured for Margaret to step forward.

Elizabeth saw the face of the old crone and gave a sharp intake of breath. There in front of her stood her mother. The secret of life and death had been there in front and inside of her the whole time.

There are certain days in your life's calendar that you will find harder than others. It might be the birthday of your loved one, it might be your own birthday or the annual recurrence of the anniversary of their death. Each year that I experience these anniversaries, they feel different. To do justice to the memory of our mum and the positive relationship we had with her, my sister and I have started to try to turn the energy of these days around. On Mum's birthday, we always try to do something nice in her name. It might be a day out to somewhere she loved, or a meal in her favourite restaurant.

If you know there is a significant date looming, try to clear your calendar a little. Perhaps take a day off, give yourself a duvet day or plan to do something nurturing. If there are friends or relations who live near you, don't face that day alone.

A year ago, I decided I wanted to change the associations with the anniversary of my mother's death. I had decided to bring a dog into my life as a companion, so I arranged it so that on New Year's Eve, the night before the anniversary, I collected the puppy. This seems to have had quite a positive impact, as now I can think of that day as Scout the spaniel's coming-home day. It doesn't mean I have forgotten my mum, not by a long shot, but she would have wholeheartedly approved.

TRY THIS: A RITUAL IN MEMORY OF YOUR LOVED ONE

This ritual is designed so that it can be performed alone or, better still, with one or two people. You might find comfort in being able to connect with others in this way. So do ask a family member or a friend or two to join you and you can divide up the lines of the readings. It is helpful if they knew the loved person also, as we will be inviting you all to share a treasured memory. If they didn't know your loved one, then it helps if you can offer them a favourite story to share.

You will need:

* A black altar cloth
* Photographs and mementos of your loved one
* A small offering dish or bowl in front of each photograph
* A white candle
* A black candle
* A candle or tea-light holder for each ritual participant
* A glass or cup of your loved one's favourite tipple (preferably something that won't go cold, or that you can keep warm)
* A small portion of their favourite food
* A censer, a charcoal disc or two and some of the incense you made in the previous ritual
* A bell

Begin by creating an altar space to celebrate your loved one, ideally in the northern sector of your room. Cover a table with a black altar cloth or scarf and decorate it with the photographs and mementos. Select photos that are anchored in a positive memory – when your loved one was well, healthy and doing something they loved with you. Perhaps a day out or a significant birthday celebration. Place the black candle on one side of the photos and the white candle on the other.

Before you begin, spend some time in the ritual space, tidying and cleaning it to prepare it for the ritual. Air the space out so that the room feels fresh and clean. Light the censer and burn some of the incense. Dress in something comfortable and soft that makes you feel cosy. Light the candles and sit for a moment at the altar. If you are performing the ritual in a group, each take a moment or two to sit and connect to the photographs of the loved one.

Start the ritual by placing your feet firmly on the ground and taking three deep breaths in, feeling the air filling your lungs completely. On the out-breath, allow a little sigh to escape your lips. On the in-breath, feel the strength of the divine presence of your loved one filling the space around you. Then, when you feel ready, ring the bell three times and say these words:

> As the bell rings in the passage of time,
> We stand on the sacred earth.
> As unseen as the mystery of death,
> Our beloved [insert name] has passed beyond
>   the gates of eternity,
> To a place we cannot follow
> Until our own time has come.

If you are on your own, carry on speaking the words below. If you have others with you, let them all take a turn to speak. The second person says:

> We, who would seek the secret of death, must
>   trust our dreams,
> For in them is hidden the gate to eternity. Since
>   we cannot find the way,
> We call upon the gods of Life and Death – Osiris,
>   Jesus, Shiva, Baldr, Dionysus, Cernunnos
> *To bear witness to our ritual, given in love to the*
>   *memory of* [insert name]

We gather on the edge of night, on the edge
    of love,
On the edge of our dreams, on the edge of life.
Even as the river and sea are one,
In the depth of our hopes and desires,
Lies our silent knowledge of the beyond.
We open our hearts wide with love to the
    memory of [insert name].

Ring the bell three times again and place a small pinch of incense on the charcoal. As the smoke goes upwards, Person One says:

As the smoke travels skywards and reaches out
    into the beyond
Let it carry a message of love to our beloved
    [insert name].

Person Two says:

We call upon all our beloved ancestors to hold us
    and [insert name]
Safely in their arms until we are reunited again.

Person Three says:

We loved you in life, [insert name].
So, we gather to share your stories and songs.
Draw near, beloved, and hear our circle
    of dreaming,
For it is you we dream of, you we remember.

Gather around the altar. Sit if you can, and each take time to share a story of the beloved person who has died. Take your time to enjoy the telling. Cry if you need to, laugh if you can. As each person's telling draws to an end, toast the person who has died by sharing a taste of their favourite food and a sip of their favourite tipple. When everyone has shared their story, take the food and drink that are left and leave a small portion in the offering bowl on the altar.

End the ritual with their favourite song or poem or an excerpt from their favourite story – something that they loved in life, or that you shared with them.

Person Two then says:

> We would know the secret of death.
> Must seek it in the heart of life.

Person One adds:

> And so we continue our journey through life,
> Knowing we were enriched by the presence of
>   [insert name].

Person Three continues:

> We loved you in life, [insert name],
> Just as we love you beyond death
> When our time comes, you will meet us at
>   the gate.
> And we will be reunited once more.
> Until then, may our loving thoughts carry
>   you forward
> On your journey into what lies beyond.

Ring the bell three times again to end the ritual. Make sure you now go and do something very physical to ground yourselves – take a walk in nature, eat a meal together, dance, embrace each other. Take a moment to acknowledge that time may not take away the grief for the loss of your late beloved, but that you have companions in life who are there to hold you and console you.

Our next journey through the woods in winter takes us in search of other endings you may have encountered – the end of friendships, or the end of a love affair. Soon we will be seeing signs of spring again beneath the trees – the new, green shoots of ferns and nettles, the leaf spears of snowdrops and daffodils. The mornings will grow lighter, and the woods will call you out to spring. Until then, we have one more grove to visit to take us through winter's embrace.

CHAPTER TWO

THE JOURNEY TO THE END OF THE AFFAIR

I know what my heart is like
Since your love died:
It is like a hollow ledge
Holding a little pool
Left there by the tide,
A little tepid pool,
Drying inward from the edge.

Edna St Vincent Millay

TAROT CARD: The Tower or the Three of Swords

Divorce, like death, is one of those life events that always leaves people scrabbling for an apology. 'I am sorry,' people will tell me if it comes up in conversation that I am divorced (and usually I only tell them because they have asked me if I am married). 'I'm not!' is usually my response, at which point they hurriedly change the subject.

The end of a relationship can be awful to go through. You may be left grappling with a sense of failure, of grief at the loss of the relationship or the potential you once thought it had, and the numb sense of shock that sometimes washes in in the immediate aftermath of a catastrophic event. But sometimes it can turn out to be the best decision you ever made (if you were the ender) or the kindest thing someone ever did for you (if you were the endee). As with the grief that comes from a death, it's hard to show you a photograph of what your path through this area of the woods will look like, as every relationship is different. There will be, however, landmarks in common. And it is those that we'll be navigating here.

Some relationships end with a bang, and some like a balloon losing its air as it flies around the room emitting a flatulent noise. And, of course, it is not always a romantic relationship that is ending. You might be about to call time on a platonic friendship if you feel your boundaries have been crossed one too many times, or perhaps there is a family member with whom a relationship is just no longer viable after much effort and pain. The thing to remember – and I can't emphasise this enough – is that you cannot change other people, you can only affect transformation in your own life. Sometimes you really do reach the end of a journey, with your path diverging from another's. The truth is, however, that I have never experienced a relationship ending that didn't leave me better off in the long run. But let's not race ahead. Let's begin by pausing on the path again, and meeting with Elizabeth, who is now on a different kind of journey.

PREPARING FOR THE JOURNEY: THRESHOLDS, LIMINAL SPACES AND THE COMMITMENT TO CHANGE

Elizabeth stood at the window of her tower room, watching the storm. Many years had passed since she had returned to the world of the living from her descent into the underworld. She had met a man, and fallen in love, but things were not going well. Time had become wearisome, and many cares furrowed her brow. There was a low rumble of thunder that echoed through the valley as if it were contained within a punch bowl. Elizabeth counted silently in her head, 'One, two, three, four', before the valley was lit up by the sheet lightning, momentarily turning night to day and confusing all of her senses. Her heart gave a little leap, partly through fear of what it would reveal, but partly through the sheer exhilaration of watching the storm. A fox shrieked in the night, and she felt the need to open her door and welcome all the wild creatures inside for safe refuge.

Another low rumble. This one so low she could sense it vibrating through her body before she heard it. One, two, three, crack. An oak in the valley was struck and burst into flames.

Before you start making plans for the future and the amazing things that will doubtless come your way, let's pause for a minute and consider how you know you've reached the end of the road with somebody in your life. There's the fear of getting the decision wrong, for a start. What happens if you end a relationship, and then regret it? It's worth spending some time thinking about boundaries and thresholds at this point. If you're in a relationship with someone who is repeatedly crossing your boundaries – for example, they might be continually unfaithful when you expect monogamy, or they might be stealing or gambling away your money, or being violent or verbally abusive to you or others, using drugs or alcohol or simply not thinking of your best interests when they make decisions without you – you are going to reach a threshold moment sooner rather than later.

It can feel overwhelming and frustrating when someone is repeatedly crossing your line, promising changes and not delivering. To be frank, if you are waiting for someone else to transform, but no alteration has occurred despite repeated conversations, it's unlikely it will come. Promises without actions are empty gestures, and if a person thinks they may have 'got away with it' up until now, then they are unlikely to be motivated to change. Also, be prepared for the fact that if you threaten to pull the plug, they will more than likely start bargaining with you and promising you the earth, but it still doesn't mean they will change. One ex-partner finally confessed to me that he was used to promising me things to get me to calm down and, once the dust had settled, he went right back to doing what he had done before, safe in the knowledge that the storm had passed for now.

Having worked in an addictions charity for over twenty years, I do not doubt that people *can* change – but the motivation has to come from within themselves, not outside, and no amount of pressure from you will help. Making significant changes in your life can be hard work, if not brutal, and it requires a commitment to yourself that is second to none.

A threshold, as the name suggests, is, in psychological terms, the amount of stimulus you need to transition from one state into another. It is the motivator that helps you to cross an irreversible boundary (for more about boundaries, see Chapter Three). You are passing through a gateway from which there is no going back; making that step means you will never be the same person again. In Wicca those boundaries are sacred places – we know that while they are not visible to the naked eye, they can be felt. We willingly and knowingly cross the boundary between 'the worlds of men and gods' when we enter a circle or sacred space. We honour those threshold moments by marking them out, and by naming them as we step between the worlds. In nature, those boundaries can be intensely fertile or places rich in biodiversity, and they are often blocked off in some way to prevent injury or damage to property, but this creates a safe space for nature to thrive without the presence of human intervention. In cities these places are often referred to as the 'edgelands' – those fertile strips of apparent wasteland, for example the banking along railway lines or the fenced-off areas between industrial and domestic spaces. From the window of a train, you might see a plethora of species living undisturbed –a buddleia bush covered in butterflies, or a fox dozing in the afternoon sunshine. In our coastal areas, those interstitial spaces mark the boundary between the land and the seashore, where salt water meets fresh water and streams roll down into the ocean. In woodland they are the clearings where we might discover a patch of ripening blackberries or sloes.

At a threshold, even if this was not a threshold of your choosing, you are momentarily in a liminal space. You are no longer the 'old you', though you are perhaps not sure who the 'new you' will be; you might start to see where the berries grow, even if, in winter, the birds have stripped the bushes bare. You might want to make a mental note of them, to revisit them in spring and see what delights have flowered there, or in autumn to see what riches you can glean. In my diary, I had described a threshold moment such as this:

1 June
I feel strange, and I feel unsettled – like I'm in a holding space, waiting to find out the missing information that will tell me what I'm to do next, where I am to go. It's a really weird feeling, somewhat akin to not knowing, but I am more restless as I know it's going to involve a big change.

Within a healthy relationship, when a threshold moment happens, there is the capacity to adapt and change to allow for the new growth that comes with one partner crossing into a different part of the woods. However, when it is the behaviour of a loved one that's pushed you to this precipice, the likelihood is that you are going to be leaving them behind and striking out on your own. Reaching this moment can feel frightening and uncertain, but, remember, the threshold is the stimulus that gives us the energy to make the change. Sometimes we need that burst of anger or grief or frustration to make it happen.

9 April
I feel angry *and* all over the place today. I got so angry today I burst into tears and had to leave the office and walk

around the lake. But it gave me a really important insight. I've really struggled with boundary setting most of my adult life. Why? Because I modified myself to contain the anger. I spent my adult years suppressing the anger and trying not to get angry. But it's anger that helps you to set boundaries. To say no, enough is enough.

Ignoring these inner voices that are telling you that you're worth more than this and that you deserve better can ultimately leave you ill and depleted. So, if you think you might have reached the threshold point, and you're unsure about what to do, it's very important you take the time to listen to yourself and check in with how you are feeling. It is perfectly valid to be feeling any of the stages of grief at this point, and it might be a good time to seek some advice (if you can) from a neutral party. And remember, it's not selfish to make the best decision for you. Sometimes in this life, the only knight in shining armour we can expect is ourselves, and if you aren't willing to fight for yourself, who else will?

TRY THIS: CROSSING THE THRESHOLDS

So, you think you might have reached the end of the road with a particular relationship, but how do you know? In all good faith, there is no golden rule. However, your inner self will tell you what is going on for you, even if your conscious self is in denial and pretending nothing is wrong. If you're not sure, there are a few areas of your life I would invite you to pay a little extra attention to, as they may start to reveal clues.

It's often the case that, at end of a lengthy relationship, we're afraid we won't be able to make it in the outside world on our own. In my case, my inner F.E.A.R.s (false expectations that appear real) were telling me I couldn't afford to live alone, and that surely the situation with my current partner wasn't so bad. Looking back, however, four specific areas gave the game away. These are the questions I would like to share with you and suggest you begin exploring in your journal:

- What is your favourite song currently? What is the predominant music you're listening to? If it is music with lyrics, what do the lyrics say?

As a very clear example, my sister noted that, while I was still living with one ex-partner and pretending everything was fine, I kept telling her how much I loved a song by Kate Nash called 'Dick Head'! Our unconscious minds struggle with some of the logical aspects of language, but they respond well to music.

- What is your body telling you?

Sometimes, our unconscious minds speak to us through physical responses. Because the unconscious can't use language, it can't simply tell you, 'I want to get out now', so it will use the physical body to convey its discomfort.

For example, in my private diaries of one break-up, I wrote the following:

> Sunday 17 March
> Turbulent times, and my back has responded accordingly. I felt it slip in Pilates on Thursday and I'm back to being lopsided again. The muscles are in spasm, and I find myself wincing at every movement. X is still being a problem – texting, calling, crying, getting angry, begging, etc. I'm still standing firm.

My body was responding to the situation in a way that I could no longer ignore. If you ever doubt the link between the emotional body and the physical body, there was one final detail that convinced me. Following that break-up, I kept being attracted to very similar types of people. I hadn't yet dealt with my iffy blueprint – the conditioning we all learn from childhood that can lead us into making the same choices over and over again. Every time I could see the seeds of the old relationship blueprint playing out once more, my body very helpfully decided to speak loud and clear. In a later diary entry, I wrote:

> 11 June
> My sciatica has reared its charmingly painful head again – to remind me I need to change who I choose to be with. The pain only began to show signs of retreat when I acknowledged that I can't afford to go back to another relationship like that, because if I did, what would have been the point in fighting my way out of the last one?

- When you think of the future, what do you see?

At the end of some of my significant relationships, I realised that when I thought about the future, there was no colour at all. It was monochrome and foggy, a slate-grey city sky, with an oppressive layer of thick, heavy winter cloud. When I think of my future now, by contrast, I feel a sense of excitement for potential adventures – I see sunshine, green foliage, sparkling water, new things to encounter. If your future with a new person feels as grey as the last, clearly something needs to change.

- When you talk to other people about the life you live with your partner, what expressions do you see reflected on their faces?

Bearing in mind that you could be experiencing a coercive or controlling relationship, where you struggle to see the truth of the situation, another killer clue I had was when I began noticing the reactions that others unwittingly let slip when I spoke with them. For example, I remember one conversation where I was telling a friend about something my ex-husband had said about me. I saw a look of pure horror pass over her face, until she remembered to try to wear a more neutral expression. Another friend suddenly started talking to me about divorce before I'd really worked out that was the destination I was heading for. At this point, the tarot card that kept showing up for me was the Devil. Despite its fearsome reputation, this card doesn't point to Satan himself (he is not acknowledged in Wicca, but is a creation of Christianity and Islam). Instead, it indicates an addiction at work, or a position of entrapment where only you can free yourself (the chains worn around the neck of the two people depicted could easily be lifted off if they chose).

The end of a relationship can severely affect everything you do – you might be facing physiological problems, safety concerns, a challenge to your sense of being loved or lovable or belonging in a family unit, as well as the fact that your self-esteem has probably been taking quite a battering over the last few months or years. It is important to remember that this too shall pass. In tarot, the Wheel of Fortune card speaks of better things coming, but it also reminds us that everything in life keeps moving. It might feel as if you're stuck in an awful situation, but sooner or later the wheel will turn again and move you on to better things.

Oh, and by the way, in case you were wondering, obviously I managed to live very well on my own.

READING THE MAP: THE TOWER CARD AND OTHER ENDING ARCHETYPES

Something in Elizabeth told her it was time to leave. Just then, the heavens opened, releasing a torrent of hot, huge raindrops, and the fire gave in and retreated. She knew that all the wisdom said never go out into the heart of a thunderstorm, especially if you are going to be around tall buildings or trees, but here was the thing. She was standing in the room at the uppermost reaches of the tower, the tallest structure for miles around, surrounded by trees that reached up to grasp her hands at the window. If anything made her vulnerable, it was her elevated position.

She picked up the turquoise silk bag from the table beside the window and slid the deck of cards out from their cocoon. 'What wisdom do I need to know now, on this night of change?' she whispered, and allowed the cards to run through her fingers as she shuffled them. She placed three of them on the table, face down. Past, present, future. Then one by one she turned them over.

Past – the Nine of Swords. The figure on the card looked so familiar, she could almost have been Elizabeth herself, sitting up in bed, her head in her hands, as the nine swords played out their fearful thoughts above her head. So many times, she had sat up in the night like this, her thoughts bombarding her with anxiety.

Present – the Tower. Elizabeth let out a sigh of exasperation. Of course, it was the lightning-struck tower, cloven in two, bodies falling from the uppermost window. She had never noticed before how much the tower on the card looked like the one she stood in now.

Future – the Hermit. The cloaked figure held aloft a lantern, shin-ing its light into the darkness, drawing animals towards it. It was time for Elizabeth to take herself away from other people for a while. To find somewhere to hear her own thoughts, to discover her own wisdom, to care for herself. Once upon a time she would have dreaded the thought of being alone, but now she knew this was just what she needed.

'Help! I need some relationship archetypes!' This was the message I sent out to my new partner and my best friend and her husband at six o'clock on the morning I was writing this chapter. Bearing in mind that we are all bookworms, we couldn't between us come up with a single archetypal story of a relationship break-up that hap-pened in a 'healthy' way. They were all tales of revenge, fury and death, from the love triangle of Arthur, Guinevere and Lancelot to the extramarital affairs of Zeus and Hera (and her various forms of revenge), from the *Mabinogion* to the *Poetic Eddas* and the Homeric hymns.

If anything, the relationship archetypes here are anti-archetypes, or ways that you *shouldn't* behave if you're experiencing the end of an affair (although we don't do 'should' and 'shouldn't' here either). That's not to say break-ups are easy, obviously, but I couldn't identify a deity who rules over divorce, although there are plenty that rule over death and marriage. In mythos, no boundaries were clearly stated nor interventions staged nor relationship counselling sessions embarked upon.

There are tales of devotion that go beyond the grave – such as the story of Isis, who searches to the ends of the earth to bring back the dismembered parts of her husband Osiris and then uses magic to piece them back together. Or Orpheus, who journeys to the underworld to find his lost love, Eurydice. Yet none of these stories exactly give us hope of a brighter day. Nor do they provide us with a blueprint of how to behave, unless we take them to serve as a warning. They do reveal, however, the extent of the dysfunction that relationships can take, and the complications that have ensued across millennia when they are allowed to run their course unchecked and unmanaged. We need to find another way to conduct our adult relationships, so that they can be both fulfilling and nurturing. It might surprise you to know that tarot can help us do this.

In the tarot, we start to see a few clues when we look to our readings. If you do a reading for yourself when you're contemplating an ending, you might well see the familiar signs emerging. The Tower may appear – the card that indicates a sudden lightning strike that splits the tower to its very foundations. You might also see the Three of Swords piercing a red heart, the sign of a betrayal, of heartbreak and of loss. None of these is exactly cheery in its outlook but, as with any rock-bottom moment, it's a good foundation from which to build again.

If you are struggling to see the relevance of such tools, let me just say that I don't see tarot as a 'fortune-telling' method to show you the fixed and certain future. I see it as a device to help you explore the misty areas of a situation you might not be consciously aware of. Each of my endings showed up in the cards long before they happened, and through a gradual awakening I was able to put measures in place that would empower me to take the necessary steps when the time was right. Take your time, and don't rush this, unless your life is at stake. As I've stated earlier in this chapter, your experiences will get better. The future is hopeful and full of colour: you just have to allow it to exist as a possibility.

TRY THIS: PULL AN ARCHETYPE CARD FOR YOURSELF

Before we get into the business of doing more complex tarot readings for ourselves, I am going to invite you to dip a toe in the tarot water by pulling just one card. You can use this each morning as a daily guidance practice to help you navigate difficult times, or as a way of gradually learning the cards.

You will need:

* A pack of cards – either tarot or other oracle cards
* It will also help to have the guidebook for your cards.

Sit quietly somewhere you won't be disturbed and shuffle the cards thoroughly. In a new pack the cards will all be in order, so it's important you shuffle them well to give the opportunity to surprise you. My tarot teacher Phoenix has people 'skoosh' the cards at this point – spreading them across a tabletop and mixing them up with their hands to make sure they are completely randomly arranged when you put them back together. Once you have skooshed, gather the cards back in and start to shuffle them once more. As you do, think about what it is you want the cards to show you but, rather than form a question, perhaps form a statement of gratitude in your imagination, for example:

> Thank you, cards, for showing me what I need to know about X today. It feels good knowing you are there to help guide me.

When you are happy that you have shuffled enough, place the deck down on the table in front of you, split it into three using your non-dominant hand (i.e. your left hand if you are right-handed). Place the three piles back together in any random order you like and, again using your non-dominant hand, turn the top card over.

Before you dive into the guidebook, spend a few moments looking at the design on the card. What does it remind you of? How does the illustration tell you a story about the archetype of your own life and relationship? If you knew the answer, what would it be? It's a good idea to write each card down in your diary and reflect back on it at the end of the day. How did the meaning of that card manifest for you in the real world today?

CHARTING YOUR COURSE: TAKE COURAGE, DEAR HEART

Elizabeth made up her mind quickly. She put the cards back in their silken pouch, and grabbed her soft leather bag, tucking her most treasured items inside: her notebook and pen, her mother's locket, her map of the woods and the little turquoise silk bag that contained her tarot cards. Everything she would need to help her navigate in the world. She needed to be gone before he returned home for the night – the man of wrath who looked at her with such disapproval these days. She did not want to explain why her so-called irrational feelings were so compelling, and she did not want to have to compromise any more. She wanted to seek relief in the green, arboreal world. To find somewhere quiet and small that could be hers alone. She wanted to find sanctuary among the tall trunks, the moss and the bracken. She wanted to create a space that would nurture her and the beings that would seek her out. It was time to break free.

One of the things that helped me to transform my life completely – because, to reassure you, it *is* possible – was starting to pay attention to the voice in my head. You may know that voice: the inner critic, the one that very often gives you a running commentary, including a harsh value judgement of everything you do. If you've grown up with an overly critical role model in your life from an early age, you're more likely to have a critical commentary going on in your own mind that stays with you long into adulthood, but it is possible to change this. When I started to pay attention to the tone of that voice and the language it used, I was quite horrified. If a partner had spoken to me in that manner, I would have been quicker to realise the need to leave, but then you can't easily leave yourself, can you? In my neuro-linguistic programming (NLP) training – a branch of psychology where I started to learn the user manual for my own brain and behaviour – we were encouraged to turn that voice, boggart-like, into the voice of someone very silly who made us laugh. It helped to take the sting out of the inner critic and turn it into something more supportive.

TRY THIS: A WALK WITH YOUR INNER VOICE

Take a walk in nature, preferably alone, as this allows you to be in a state of solitude with your thoughts. Perhaps take a notebook with you if you find it helps to write down what you are thinking.

Think back to an issue that's bothered you in recent weeks and how you handled it. What was it about that situation that you found difficult? Was it the behaviour of someone else, or how you responded to it that caused your sense of unease? If that same situation were to play out again, how would you handle it differently?

If you are someone who does experience an inner voice, I would invite you to focus in on that voice when you play back the scenario. What is its tone? Is it friendly or harsh? Whose voice do you hear in your head when you play back a particular situation? Does it belong to someone you know? If you were to put a name to it, who would it be?

If you don't have that sense of an inner voice, try paying particular attention to the moments when you felt a sense of either physical or emotional discomfort. What was it about that scenario that made you feel that way? Was your perspective particularly harsh on yourself? Did you default to feeling that the situation was all your fault? Does that way of thinking about yourself remind you of anyone you know? Did someone in your life always judge you harshly, when you secretly wished they were there with unwavering support?

Often when we run into a problem with our unconscious programming, we discover that our unconscious mind was just trying to keep us safe. It sets out with good intentions, but sometimes these become a little skewed along the way. For this reason, rather than fight mean with mean, I would invite you to thank the voice lovingly for its input in trying to help you and assure it that it is safe for it to take a step back.

Now, close your eyes and take three deep breaths. Imagine the most loving person you have experienced in your life. Who made you feel safest and most cared for? If you struggle to think of a real person, it is fine to consider a fictional character at this point, as long as the sound of that person's voice is soothing, or the perspective they bring is a supportive one. Invite that person or character to step forward in your thoughts. Next, give yourself a name in your head that represents a term of endearment and invite that loving voice (which is really another aspect of yourself) to be the voice of commentary that you pay attention to going forward, or for the supportive perspective to become the one you pay attention to. For example, when I'm addressing myself in my head, I now use the term 'darling' in place of 'idiot' or any of the other insulting terms I formerly used. At first it might feel artificial, and you might need to check yourself and actively remember to keep replacing the harsh voice with the loving one and the mean words with the kind ones, but after a while it will begin to feel more natural. Each time the old critic rears its head, just thank it for its concern and reassure it, 'We've got this.'

If you really feel you've reached the end of the road in a particular relationship, it is imperative that you listen to the loving voice and become your best supporter, as this will help you to make the changes ahead.

NAVIGATING A NEW LANDSCAPE: ALONE-NESS AND FINDING WHAT YOU LOVE

Throwing her red cloak around her shoulders once more, Elizabeth placed the bag across her body. She lit the storm lantern to light the way, threw the door open, grabbed her walking staff and made her way out of the room and to the staircase.

As she reached the front door and threw it open on the night, her breath caught in her throat. Trees blew in the storm like seaweed underwater. They swayed and creaked, bent to almost unreasonable proportions by the strong wind that held them in its grasp, but still they stood, and she knew she must remain flexible, just like they were.

She looked ahead and started to pick out the beginnings of the path through the wood. She noticed, as she took each step forward, the wind began to die down, and her heart lifted a little at every step. At first it was almost imperceptible, but her gaze began to light once more on the parts of the woods that she loved the most. There, look! There was her favourite beech tree, with its copper leaves glistening in the moonlight. Perhaps there she might find some rest.

So much of our society is built around everyone being in couples that you really can start to feel like Bridget Jones in a room full of twosomes when you strike out alone. But sometimes this can be the greatest gift you give yourself. While one of your fears when ending a relationship is that you might be alone forever, let's blow the old 'there's only one person for each of us' myth out of the water – there are, in fact, any number of people out there who would be lucky to be with you (please refer to Chapter Three for more on this). However, now that we have identified our own relationship blueprints, we need to give ourselves time to rediscover and redraw them: we risk living 'Relationship Groundhog Day' until we do.

The best way to do this is to spend some time alone – ideally in nature – exploring the things you love before diving into a new relationship. By removing all the people and distractions around you for a bit, you can start to identify the form and shape of your patterns, just like a tree stripped back for winter. Learning a new pattern takes courage, an open heart and the willingness to look very honestly at some quite painful memories and to acknowledge your own part in what went wrong. This can only work well if you give yourself time alone. What's important for you right now is to give yourself a little space to find out (or remember) what it is that you love. How can we expect to find happiness if we have forgotten what makes us happy? Women particularly are trained to adapt to the needs of a partner; to avoid doing this again, it's crucial you give yourself a bit of space to see what flows in, or rather, give yourself a season of winter so that you can see what grows back in the spring.

So, take yourself off to your nearest body of water, or your local nature reserve, and sit for a while by the water or among the trees and just allow your thoughts to drift. What do the branches whisper to you in the breeze? Are they whipped about by winter storms, or do they now stand aloft in the brilliant winter sunshine? What does that remind you of in your life? What wildlife appears in front of you, and what does it symbolise to you or remind you of? What occurs to you when you sit for a while and take away the need for to-do lists and a busy schedule of meetings?

This can be a difficult thing to begin as so many of us are trained to put other people ahead of ourselves. We are taught that it is selfish to put our desires above those of others, but I am here to remind you that if you were in an aeroplane that was experiencing technical problems and the air masks were released, your instructions would be to put your own oxygen mask on first, before you start trying to help other people. You can't save anyone else on the plane if you are unconscious.

Having time alone allows you to reset your inner compass and pour strength into the trunk of your own sapling, which needs to be strong and well rooted before you join your life with somebody else's again. Some people hop from one relationship straight into another without giving themselves this reset point (I had done it from the age of sixteen to the end of my marriage at forty-five). The danger of that approach is that you are then relying on 'fate' to bring you into contact with someone nicer who will treat you well, and I don't believe that waiting for the Moirai (those ancient Greek sisters who personified destiny, with the one eye they shared between them) to weave a more beautiful tapestry for you is the answer. It also doesn't allow for the fact that, if your blueprint is skewed, the nicest person could show up in your life and you might not even realise they were there because your physical and emotional responses are trained to be attracted to the 'wrong 'uns', as mine were. Our perceptions are the filters we see the world through, and if they are focused on the wrong thing, no amount of good things will get through to your heart-space and make it in the possibilities section of the relation-shop aisle. So, do yourself a favour and give yourself a break. And don't be afraid that you will end up, Bridget Jones-like, alone and eaten by Alsatians. That's a far more likely fate if you keep making unhelpful choices for yourself. When you have started to weed out what it is you want from life and where you think you can find happiness, then it is time to write a letter to the future.

TRY THIS: A LETTER TO THE FUTURE

In the years before Covid, I was in the privileged position of teaching a group of young people, a group that we lovingly referred to as the Witchlets. The classes were themed around topics relating to Wicca but, over time, we also developed a group egregore – a shared awareness of a common interest – and the feeling of being part of a supportive community. The attendees were young, creative, often getting to grips with a number of mental health diagnoses, and in search of greater meaning in their lives. Ultimately, they taught me a lot and I'm privileged to have worked with them.

One of the exercises I remember most fondly was the 'letter to the future'. For this, I gave each person a piece of notepaper and an envelope and encouraged them to write a letter to their future selves. I then took the letters, put them away and posted them back to them a year later. In a superb twist of irony, this was one of our last gatherings before the pandemic took hold and scattered us all to the four corners of the earth.

There are websites that offer this service: you can write a note, and then set a timer for when you want to receive it – for example, in six months, a year, three years, five years or ten years. If that all seems a little technologically complicated, you can create a do-it-yourself version at home.

Obviously, it's an exercise in imagination, but it was one of the most powerful tasks we did. The only restriction I gave my students was that their letter needed to be written in gentle, loving and encouraging language.

I would now like to invite you to write a letter to yourself in the future about your hopes for a better life.

You will need:

* A piece of lovely writing paper and an envelope
* A pen that you enjoy writing with
* Somewhere safe to tuck the letter away
* A reminder system – for example, a reminder on your phone that pops up in a year's time and tells you where to look for the letter

Find a quiet space, where you will be undisturbed. Focus for a moment on your breath, allowing your body to settle, and then put your pen to paper. As I said, the rules of the letter are that you must use positive and encouraging language.

If you were to receive a letter in the future from your past self, what would you like it to say? What advice would you give yourself (if any)?

If it helps to have an example, my letter read:

6 January 2020

Darling Bex,

Well, it's been quite a year, hasn't it? I have to say I have no expectation of where you will be this time next year when this letter finds you. However, I have absolute faith in you. Will you be in London? Will you be in Devon? Will you be somewhere warmer? I hope you will have had a marvellous year with many adventures. Will you be Doctor Bex? Will you be teaching full time? Will you be single? Or will you have found an emperor worthy of you? All I ask is that you continue to do the things that inspire you with the people that love you. And know, I and all of our ancestors are immensely proud of you. Do also remember this letter was written in a room with a group of people who were intently writing their own letters, absorbed in what they were doing, and in utter silence. And you did that. You brought them together.

All my love,

Bex

PS If you've found us an emperor, I bet he's fabulous.

If you have worked through some of the activities in this chapter, or have already experienced the ending of a relationship, it's important to give yourself the time to mark the ending, to honour it and let go. In Western society, we are used to having rites of passage that mark certain key points in life – births, marriages and deaths – but we are less practised at knowing what to do with the in-between points, those liminal spaces in which we've left one state behind but haven't yet transitioned to the new one. The following ritual is designed to help you do that. Afterwards, it will be time to move on into spring and explore the New Relationships chapter. But for now, let's honour that ending and the ongoing transformation you are undergoing.

TRY THIS: A RITUAL TO MARK A RELATIONSHIP ENDING

You will need:

* A candle of any colour that appeals to you. It can be blue, green, black, red or gold – it doesn't matter, as long as you like it
* A candleholder that appeals to you

* A toothpick
* Your notebook and pen to make notes at the end if you want to

Feel free to carry out this ceremony with a loved one, a good friend or a group of people who have helped support you. If you can perform the immersion in water exercise (see page 230) beforehand by way of preparation, all the better, particularly if it's in a bath at home and you are intending to do this ritual at home.

This ritual is adapted from a visualisation exercise called Hoʻoponopono that I was taught by David Shephard of the Performance Partnership. It's taken from Hawaiian Huna practices and is designed as an exercise in letting go.

I would invite you to find a space that is comfortable and safe. Close your eyes and focus on your breath for a few moments. I'd like you to visualise a stage being lit in front of you. Picture it however you want – either as a bare stone amphitheatre, or a stage in the round, or one with curtains and wings. Imagine the spotlight hitting a central point on the stage. Invite the person with whom you are experiencing the relationship ending to walk onto the stage and into the spotlight. Look at them for a moment with loving eyes. Try to remember the positive parts of your relationship, and anything you may have learned from it. Begin to talk through with them the ending that you are sharing, and why it is necessary. Acknowledge that you have reached the end of your journey with them but that, for both of you, life will continue along different paths.

Say to them, 'I am sorry. I forgive you.' Then tell them, 'Thank you', 'I love you' and that you release them. Send them into the world with love.

If you experience any hint that the release has not yet happened, you can repeat the process and visualise silvery strands of energy, connecting your body to theirs, shining softly in the light of the theatre. Then from out of your pocket imagine that you have taken a good sturdy pair of scissors (as we can in our imaginations!). As the silvery tendrils float in the air in front of you, feel free to take the scissors in your hand and snip through every last one of them. Watch them as they melt into the air and vanish, and say once more, 'I release you with love.'

When you are ready, open your eyes and take up the candle and the toothpick. Use the toothpick to carve your initials onto the candle, and add something that symbolises your new life to you. It might be a single word – freedom, release, autonomy – or it might be a dragonfly or another symbol that is meaningful to you. When you are ready, hold the candle to your heart and picture that new life in your imagination. What will you see, feel, hear, touch and taste when it is here? When you have that image in your mind, say the words, 'And so it is', place the candle in a holder and light it. Focus on the growing strength of its light as it pierces the darkness. Leave it burning for as long as you want to, either for short bursts over the next few days, to remind you of the positive change that is coming to you in the months and years ahead, or letting it burn through all at once.

Each time you extinguish it, just say the words, 'As above, so below', to indicate to your unconscious mind that while the candle may not be burning in the physical world, it's still lit in your imagination.

Now go and eat something to ground yourself, keep well hydrated in the coming hours and look forward to the incremental improvements that will emerge once you have made the move towards a big change in your life.

Of course, not all relationship endings are bad experiences. Sometimes the ending of a situation that's caused much anguish marks liberation. When I had that last break-up, one friend noted that he thought I looked very calm and expansive on it, while other people remarked that I had changed from being someone who wore only grey or black to dressing in colours and having a spring in my step. If your own perception has got confused by what someone is telling you, don't be afraid to look to your friends to tell you what they see.

There is a reason I themed this book by seasons. Winter can sometimes feel tough, but there's also a sense in which wintering is essential to our physical, mental and spiritual well-being. Sometimes it's necessary for us to withdraw into ourselves a little, to shut out the world, to draw our sap inward and enable our focus to go inward too. You may feel as if the wind is battering at your door and, if you venture outside, the cold is biting and the ground is hard beneath your feet, but in nature in winter life is merely pausing to catch its breath. It's not dead, it's just sleeping: before you know it, it will be time for spring and the new awakenings that brings.

PART TWO

SPRING IN THE WOODS

Ah come, come quickly, spring! . . .
Come and lift us to our end, to blossom,
bring us to our summer,
we who are winter-weary in the winter of the world . . .
Come and cajole the gawky colt's-foot flowers.
Come quickly, and vindicate us
against too much death.

D. H. Lawrence

THEMES: Signs of life, new beginnings, blowing the cobwebs away, new inspiration, creativity
PLANET: Mercury
ELEMENT: Air
DIRECTION: East
TIME OF DAY: Dawn

Spring has finally crept into the corners of the woods, shooing away the deep arboreal slumber. It kisses away the tears of grief and sadness, and plants a seed of hopefulness in our hearts for something better that may be just around the corner. Spring may not be the quick, bounding hare until it gains its momentum around the moment of the vernal equinox – 20 March or so – but in its earliest murmurings, around the pagan festival of Imbolc on 2 February, it beckons us back into the woods with the promise of adventures yet to come. The mornings may still be dark, the earth hard and there may still be some bite in the air, but look closely and you'll find new growth pushing its way up through the earth that wasn't there yesterday.

Each time another spring comes to these woods I feel a sense of inward relief that all is as it should be; no matter what challenges the winter has brought, and even if the spring continues to hold trials, things are changing. Spring brings light to balance the darkness, flowers are beginning to bloom and animals such as hedgehogs are emerging from hibernation and becoming active. Crocuses and snowdrops are pushing their bright spears above the hardened earth and unfurling their pretty heads; the green and white of the snowdrops contrast with the yellow, orange and purple of the crocuses, and, in among it all, farmers are starting to prepare their fields for planting as ploughing begins and the earliest lambs are born.

By spring equinox, daffodils and primroses have joined the parade and other plants start to appear on the outer lining of the paths into the woods – with protective nettles sprouting among the ditches, and cleavers, otherwise known as goosegrass, catchweed bedstraw or sweetheart, reminding us to cleave to that which we love most. Then the ammonite spears of bracken – once used for thatching and to deter witches – and ferns, the symbol of new life and new beginnings, begin to unfurl. The first leaves to emerge on the trees are the early hawthorn or whitethorn, whose later blossoms of early summer are an ancient symbol of sexual virility and love. Early white blossom appears on the blackthorn, which yields sloes in autumn. Hawthorn leaves come first, before the blossom, while blackthorn generates confetti blossom first, quickly fading to bare branches, before the leaves unfold.

In keeping with the season, the life changes we will visit in this chapter are new beginnings; the blossoming of hope, while lovely, can also spell disruption and changes to the quiet order of life. Even the arrival of something new and golden can make us pause and question what we thought we knew. We will examine the beginnings of a new relationship, and the (occasional) trials of surviving and thriving in a family environment. This section will also contain journaling exercises using divinatory tools as a support, activities involving the natural world and rituals to punctuate the changes that come with springtime themes.

CHAPTER THREE

THE JOURNEY THROUGH NEW RELATIONSHIPS

I seem to have loved you in numberless
forms, numberless times . . .
My spellbound heart has made and
remade the necklace of songs,
That you take as a gift, wear round
your neck in your many forms,
In life after life, in age after age, forever.

Rabindranath Tagore

TAROT CARD: The Lovers or the Ace of Cups

I never thought that in the approach to my fifth decade I'd be beginning a new life. It wasn't a twist in the woodland path I'd anticipated. Maybe it's the expectation from our younger selves that everything will be sorted by this point, and yet here I am, trying to navigate the complications and delights of a fresh relationship without the aid of a 'how it works' manual.

If you are in the delicious agony of a new relationship, your emotions might also be all over the place. Don't be surprised if at turns you feel bewitched (that would be the dopamine and norepinephrine in your brain starting to kick in), confused by what's going on and, at times, even sad. When you start a new relationship, there are all sorts of things you must let go of and grieve for: your single status, past relationships, past choices that weren't necessarily in your best interests. Your life is transforming again.

All in all, it can be a heady time, with your heart driving you onwards through woods that suddenly feel full of activity and new life. But it's good to build in some thinking time, too. Don't be afraid to slow things down, to take a walk through the physical woods (not just the metaphorical ones) and complete a grounding or clarifying exercise from this chapter. It's not wrong to enjoy the high that new love can bring, but we can remind ourselves to be cautious about making potentially reckless decisions at this time (says the woman who has made plenty of reckless decisions around love to spare you the same).

I am often guided in my writing by asking myself, 'What would I have wanted to know when setting off on this particular path through the woods?' What advice would I give to my younger self, and what were the challenges and pitfalls? I am going to start with the question so many of us ask as we consider moving towards a relationship . . .

READING THE MAP: WHERE IS MY TWIN FLAME?

In time the imperfect goddess found her days took on a deep sense of peacefulness and purpose. She remained each night, curled up beneath the beech tree. Each morning she would walk down to the river that carved its way through the valley, and slip into the cool waters, allowing the current to carry away the hurts of her life before, the harsh words and the sense of powerlessness.

Every once in a while, Elizabeth would wonder if she would ever find the right companion to keep her company through the days and nights that lay ahead. Yet she concluded that, for now, she was content to listen only to the sound of the wind trembling the leaves of the copper beech and the rustlings of the little creatures in the undergrowth. She was enjoying tending to herself, free of the wants and needs of another.

Years ago, when I was learning to read the tarot, my first test-case was a woman in her thirties who came into our classroom with an air of considerable frustration. When I asked her what she would like to get out of her reading, she replied, 'I want to know where my twin flame is. I've been looking all around – I have done the visualisations, the love spells, I have worked on myself and done all the feng shui. Where is he? He's late, and I am getting really fed up!'

After a second or two of stunned silence, in which I realised that she wasn't joking – she really *did* want to know where her twin flame or soulmate had got to – I wasn't quite sure where to start. Was it the air of desperation that was keeping him away or the aggression that was simmering below the surface? When I laid out the tarot cards, not a single one came up to indicate that a new relationship was coming down the tracks. Obvious clues would have been the Ace of Cups (indicting a new emotional beginning – your cup literally running over); the Lovers Card (which often does what it says on the tin, or suggests you have a choice coming); or the Two of Cups, with two people standing close together, bringing their cups into the picture in a suggestion of a joining. None of these cards were present in her reading, and all I could see was an indication she should go away and work on herself – focusing on the things she loved.

What is our obsession with finding a twin flame or soulmate anyway? Don't get me wrong, some couples are clearly very well matched – my own grandparents held a level of devotion to each other that saw them through a lengthy courtship, overseas postings, a world war and more than fifty years of happy marriage – but were they soulmates?

We are led to believe that soulmates are a good thing – that this is what we should all be striving for. Yet my personal creed on seeking perfection is that it doesn't exist in nature, or anywhere else known to humankind, so why do we hope to achieve it in our own lives? If we go into a relationship expecting our new love to be flawless, we are setting them up to fail: there is no way they can live up to this vision. As a wider society, we have got used to conversations that include the immortal words, 'He (or she) would be lovely, if they would just change X, Y and Z about themselves' – as if this might be a reasonable expectation. If the 'faults' you see are too great, then perhaps that person is not someone you should be in a relationship with as it's unlikely to do either of you any favours.

So where does the idea of soulmates come from? While some sources cite Samuel Taylor Coleridge, who in 1822 wrote a letter stating that 'to be happy in life . . . you must have a soulmate', the concept didn't originate in the West. Instead, it's written about in some Hindu traditions, which posit the idea of karmic connections between souls. Often the human experience is deemed one of loneliness and isolation, and we seek connection in whatever we can. Perhaps the idea of there being a twin flame for each of us relieves the aloneness a little? In nature, some species certainly mate for life – beavers, mute swans, sea horses (who have even developed an equitable relationship where the male carries the babies), barn owls and the alpha couple in a wolf pack all cleave together for a lifetime of companionship and family life. Sadly, lobsters aren't included in this list, in spite of popular mythology that they only have eyes for each other, as the males often have a harem of females. But when it comes to humans, what determines our meeting 'the one'?

People often expect a witch to believe in fate, as it is one of the things that generally gets lumped in with astrology and divination in people's imaginations, but the truth is the complete opposite. Wiccan oral tradition suggests that how we respond to key events in our lives is a matter of free will, otherwise why would we bother with magic? (The rationale is that if everything was pre-determined then magic wouldn't work anyway.) In this sense, we co-create our lives in service and in partnership with our divine allies; we are not passive, waiting for new possibilities, such as our 'soulmate', to fall into our laps. We take an active role in bringing about change. Science now concurs with this approach, with research indicating that those with a 'destiny' mindset can often experience more break-ups as, when they don't find the perfection they are expecting, they find it easier to leave the relationship than to stay and try to fix it.

Writing in *Psychology Today*, relationships expert Dr Shauna H. Springer moots the idea that 'soulmates' are not found but rather created over a long period of time. While we might meet someone and, in that heady rush of new love, be convinced they are the best thing since sliced bread, it is impossible to guarantee that they will always be our 'perfect' match since we all change and grow over time. On the flip side, however, this means that a couple, like my devoted grandparents, can become each other's twin flame over long years of partnership as they both work at the relationship and endeavour to keep it alive. The good news? There is more than one person out there for you, and more than one way to build a life together.

READING THE MAP: I (DON'T) WANT A NEW RELATIONSHIP

One day while wandering among the trees, Elizabeth found a fallen apple, just beneath the copper beech where she still slept each night. Where had it come from? she wondered. Perhaps some creature had left it there. In a rush of uncertainty, she threw the apple to one side, far into the undergrowth, not wishing to entertain the idea that there might be another person in these woods. She thought nothing more of it and yet the next day, just where she had found the apple, a peach was sitting. She looked at it in curiosity, and wondered whether to eat it this time, before again throwing it deep into the undergrowth. This was her wild wood and she didn't want to share it with anyone, especially someone who did not make their presence more fully known. Elizabeth, the imperfect goddess, had decided she was not in need of another goddess or a god, perfect or otherwise. She wanted to remain, as she was, in a state of perpetual peacefulness.

When I was single and wondered if I would ever meet someone nice, the most common advice I got from everyone around me was 'You'll meet someone when you aren't looking.' While this may seem counterintuitive, it does actually work. In the end, I decided I would focus my efforts on carving out a life I loved on my own, and then, just at the point where I had decided I really wouldn't mind if I never met anyone new or not, in walked my partner-to-be.

I am not the only witch to have fallen for this cosmic joke of 'Do not seek and ye shall find'. There's a scene in *Practical Magic*, the film of Alice Hoffman's beautiful novel, where the lead character casts a love spell that can't work – she deliberately chooses qualities that can't possibly exist in one man. Her motivation is that, due to a familial curse, love affairs around her have all ended in disaster, and so she reasons that the only way to feel safe is to cast a love spell for a man who can't exist. In my NLP classes we were always encouraged to overextend our goals, because it was better to overreach and get part way than to underreach and be disappointed. While my personal hex was my own dysfunctional blueprint rather than an actual jinx, walking out into nature one evening to seek some answers, I reasoned that there might be something in this approach.

I sat beneath a newly unfurled oak tree, feeling the solidity of the strong trunk at my backbone filling me with its strength and the fresh green of its new leaves. I thought about the qualities I would list if I were to do a love spell of my own. Even if these were very unlikely to be found in one person, I wanted to be sure that the lessons I'd learned during counselling had taken root like the tiny acorn that had turned into that big old oak tree.

- Charisma and intellect. He will match me in intelligence, wit, kindness and compassion.
- He will have a good sense of fun, adventure and humour.
- He will like watching films and reading books.
- He will understand, revere and respect the female body.
- He will have tattoos with a story to tell.
- He will encourage, support and spur me on in my endeavours, matching them with his own.
- He will be my equal in all things.
- He will be open to, if not interested in, witchcraft.
- He will listen carefully, offer advice only when asked and be wise.
- He will be fun to be with, will make my stomach fizzle and never be dull or overbearing.
- He will not seek to control me, my thoughts, my body or my comings and goings.

That might strike you as quite a shopping list, but, since I was resolved to go it alone at this point rather than be in another broken relationship, I reasoned it couldn't hurt to ask for the 'gold star' list rather than the bronze. I stopped looking for a special someone – dating apps were never going to draw me in. Instead, I resolved to focus on creating a life of my own that lit me up, doing the things I loved doing the most. This was the point at which I completely relocated my life, began living in the place I had always felt home-sick for, and finally got that four-legged furry companion to come on walks and swims with me. That switch enabled me to wipe the slate clean and start again. It enabled me to note, in October a year later:

> I'm not in love or lust with anyone. I only mention it as it's significant. This is probably the first time in history I've not been obsessed by somebody. Nobody occupies my thoughts. Nobody distracts me from my work. It's so liberating. I've reached that Zen place of being happy on my own and not really finding it a problem. I can come and go as I please, eat what I like, go where I like, I'm the ruler of my own queendom, finally.

When I was researching this chapter, I remembered that love spell and took another look at it. The magical universe always loves a little joke at our expense, and will often deliver exactly what we ask for with a little flourish and a swift kick in the pants to remind us to not take life too seriously. When I went back to that list, I realised that my new beau matched all but two items on that original anti-love spell list, which is pretty good going.

If the idea of doing spells makes you shudder in the horror of its woo-wooness, or if it makes you feel like you are 'dabbling' in things that shouldn't be dabbled with, I offer this next 'try this' in the spirit of the idea that our unconscious minds are very adept at bringing into our lives the situations and people that we prompt them to conjure. I subscribe to the view that the universe is a sentient, living, laughing being, with which we co-exist, co-creating our reality in partnership with the divine, whether you view that as nature itself or a deity of your choice. Magic only works if you take concrete steps in the real world. It is not lighting a candle and then expecting Mr or Ms Perfect to show up – you have to do something about it.

TRY THIS: A LOVE SPELL (OR AN ANTI-LOVE SPELL)

If you ever do a love spell it's important to be aware that we are not in the business of naming names. Don't even think about it. There are several reasons for this. One is that it's not good to mess with another person's free will. If you are considering using magic for something, it should only ever be something you would be prepared to do in the physical world. For example, you wouldn't force someone to be with you physically, so you don't do it magically either. It's unethical and manipulative to even consider it. Secondly, if (like me) your past choices of partners have been somewhat questionable, it's good to offer that choice to a higher power. Magic enables you to experiment with possibilities, giving you hope of a new beginning when you perhaps thought that hope was lost.

You will need:

* A glass jar with a lid
* A pink candle
* A toothpick
* Seven drops of rose essential oil
* Seven red roses (dried) or seven pinches of dried rose petals from your local herbalist
* Some pictures of relationships you admire – don't worry if they are fictional
* A red, pink or green pen (the colours pink and green are associated with the planet Venus, which governs love, while red is the colour of Mars, which rules passion and lust).
* A pink crystal – rose quartz is good, but any pink stone will do

*   Some slips of paper, large enough to write a single word or short phrase on

If you have bought the roses fresh, hang them (heads down) on a curtain rail above a radiator for a week. You want them to be dried, because if you put fresh roses in your jar they will go mouldy, and that is not the energy you are looking to create.

Carve your initials onto the candle, along with a symbol that means love to you – it may be a simple as a love heart or something less conventional such as a Celtic love knot. Place seven drops of the rose oil on the candle and rub them into the wax, paying special attention to the wick. Light the candle and appreciate its rosy glow and scent for a moment.

Next, take the slips of paper and think about the qualities you would like to find in a new partner. For example, do you want to meet a person who loves animals? Would you prefer someone who already has children or doesn't want them at all? Maybe you're looking for an adventurer or someone to make you laugh? Whatever the qualities you are seeking, write each one down on a separate slip of paper and fold it up. Place a drop of rose oil onto each and pop them into your glass jar, along with the pink crystal and the seven dried rose heads. If you want, you can pull the petals from the heads and drop them in a few at a time. With each addition to the jar, state your intention:

I call upon a love that is mine to come into my life.

Once you have placed the last item in the jar, close the lid and carefully take up the candle. Drop some of the molten wax on top of the lid, so that it can hold the candle steady. Seven drops would be good, but if it takes more, don't fret. As you place the candle on the lid, say the words, 'And so it is.'

Place the jar somewhere you can see it (for safety) and allow the candle to burn down. Then move the jar to somewhere that will let the spell and your unconscious mind work unhindered, without you getting too caught up in 'Has it worked yet?' Under your bed might be a good bet, as this is where traditional love charms were always placed. The best thing you can do now is forget about it for the time being and get on with living your life to the full.

CHARTING YOUR COURSE: LOVE IS NOT A BATTLEFIELD

The next day, while walking in the dappled green light, the imperfect goddess came across a man sitting beside the river, watching a pair of grey wagtails bobbing on the rocks. They dipped their tails against the surface of the water as it tumbled and gushed, chased each other from one stone to the next. The man was wearing forest green, almost merging into the moss-covered trees that surrounded them. His brown hair curled around his neck, and hung long beneath his shoulders.

'Morning,' the imperfect goddess murmured, with a half smile, but inwardly feeling quite resentful that someone had strode into her woods. The man looked quite at home, and carried on watching the wagtails as he raised his hand in greeting and gave her a sideways glance. Elizabeth walked on, in search of her own company once more.

The next day she saw the same man sitting in the same spot, but this time he was gazing down into the pool, watching the trout swirling. Again, he raised his hand in greeting, but Elizabeth did not linger, choosing instead to walk on to her favourite pool further along.

On the third day, he seemed to be staring off into space, not watching anything. 'Good morning,' Elizabeth said. 'It's a beautiful day.'

'Yes,' he replied. 'I'm waiting for the nuthatch to appear. I've left some food out – over there.'

He pointed to a handful of seed in a little pile on top of a rock. Lots of small birds were feeding there – the robin, the chaffinch, the wren and the blue tit. Just then, Elizabeth saw the nuthatch land, its sleek head dipping down into the seed. She admired its blue-grey feathers and its creamy underbelly for a moment, before it flew away again. When it returned, she could see the black stripe that banded its eyes as it busied itself with picking up more seed to take home.

So, you've spent time building a life for yourself, and someone marvellous has come in and filled the space that you didn't know you had. But how do you prevent yourself from throwing away all that hard work you did in creating a life you love in the first flush of a new relationship? The internet is replete with articles about the similarities between new love and a crack high. Yes, you read that right, which means it can be hard to hold onto yourself when you are tripping out on it. I have learned that it is important in the early part of a new relationship to stay as grounded as possible. That means spending as much time on the earth as possible, in my world. Walking, getting out in nature and allowing my body to breathe. That's not to say you shouldn't enjoy the fizzle and rush of the new love experience, but it is important to live in the real world too. I once spent an afternoon with a new love that had me reeling. In my journal that day, I gushed about how I had gone from a simple crush to being deliciously in love with this person, and yet reading further in that entry, I stumbled across something else:

22 March
Having come home and spent the last hour cleaning, today feels really weird. I feel like I am coming out of a spell. But aren't I supposed to be the one who does the

bewitching? So, what just happened? I was literally drunk on the romance today and it was as compelling as ever, if not more so. I feel as if I were all over the place, and very exposed. I might as well have been running around in the street in my skiddies. I am just lying on the bed, listening to music, saying to myself, 'What the hell just happened?'

What had just happened was a head-over-heels high that wasn't at all sustainable beyond the first rush of romance. That particular relationship never blossomed, as I was (thankfully) beginning to learn my patterns and realising that I was an addict of a different kind, drawn to that intense first flush of love and anyone who seemed to promise it. I was able to counteract it by grounding again – those tasks that witches do from time to time to remember that we need to remember our humble roots. You'll note that in my diary entry I mentioned spending the last hour cleaning – that is just the sort of grounding work we do in coven settings to ensure we can plant our feet firmly back on the ground, and why every third-degree high priestess needs to do the washing up from time to time.

I know some people believe that life without drama isn't really living. Yet despite the lyrics of that well-known 1980s song, love doesn't have to be a battlefield. If that's how you both get your kicks, then fair enough, but it's something in recent years I've worked hard to eradicate. That's not to say that life exists without disagreements – you can't always agree with a loved one – but setting a few parameters with any new partner will help enormously.

Often this process can feel a little bumpy – it won't always be hearts and flowers, after all – but it's important to remember that to know your boundaries you must push them a little, or at least reflect back on experiences and relationships where you felt they were stretched or broken. This might bring up a range of different emotions, including frustration, anger, sadness and a whole plethora of others, but identifying and stating what you need and where the line is for you will really help clarify and ease your way in any new relationship.

Boundary setting with a new partner doesn't mean that your shiny new relationship is doomed to fail – if anything, it probably means you're going about it the right way, as it might prevent you from crossing a threshold of no return later. So how do you know where your boundaries are?

TRY THIS: WHAT'S IMPORTANT TO YOU (LEVEL ONE)

You can either do this exercise alone and with your journal or, if you are feeling brave enough, try it with your new partner. If that feels like a step too far, and that you might take the lid off the dustbin and accidentally cause a wildfire, do it separately and then compare answers.

If you complete this together, it's important to do it in the spirit of openness – don't tailor your answers to what you think your new partner might *want* to hear. If you can share your answers honestly and without censoring them, it will help you both to know where to draw the line and will give you an early indication of where the potential issues might lie. For example, if you are steadfastly monogamous and your partner is polyamorous, you might encounter some problems.

Begin by listing your top ten uncrossable boundaries, or if that feels hard to define, think about what would be a complete deal-breaker for you (and your partner). Once you have your answers, hold on tight to them. You will need to be able to recall them when you are in the heady steps of establishing a relationship with your new beau. Keep them somewhere you will see them regularly – I find taking a photo and making them a screensaver on my phone is a great way to do this.

EMBARKING ON THE JOURNEY: THE LESSON OF THE IVY BOUGH

The man had unnerved her, but she began to get used to finding him in places around the wood. They would exchange a few words of greeting, or talk about what creatures he was looking for that day. After a while, she found she looked forward to their encounters, and then realised she was thinking about him at other times of the day. Sam, he said he was called. She allowed his name to roll around in her mouth, becoming familiar with its sound.

Over time, Elizabeth began to feel that she wanted to have some purpose in life again, aside from existing amid the trees. Now it was spring and the floor of the forest was starting to show signs of new growth. In among the trees where the bright sunlight fell, little green shoots began to appear. It was time to start painting the flowers once more, Elizabeth decided. So she went to her bag and retrieved the little set of paints and brushes, struck by how disused they had become, how dry and brittle the brushes were. She would never be able to use these paints to colour the delicate flowers. She made her way down to the river to seek solace in its passing and, once more, slipped into its cool waters and allowed her disappointment to be soothed.

One of the patterns I discovered while considering my boundaries and how I wanted to embark on any new relationship was a tendency to fix my sights on one person, and then adapt myself into becoming what I thought they were looking for. I call this 'becoming an ivy bough' – the process by which we come to bend and adapt ourselves out of shape, and tie ourselves in knots, almost without realising. It means you grow like a climbing plant, wrapping yourself around the trunk of another tree in twists and turns that would make your hair curl if you witnessed another person doing it.

I also had a tendency to spend a lot of time trying to read the subtext in any given situation. There are lots of articles online about 'empaths': supposedly 'special' people who are able to feel more strongly than others. Lovely as this idea is, it can be quite a risky subject, as it plays into our need to be special and set apart, which often separates us from each other, and can lead to an increased feeling of isolation. Also, what we have come to think of as 'special powers' may simply be a trauma response. Studies have shown that childhood trauma can lead us to becoming more adept at feeling our way through life. If you have grown up in a situation where someone is abusive, or irrationally angry without warning, it can often lead to a hypersensitivity to the emotional undercurrents of a situation, and a tendency to grow like ivy in order to avoid confrontation. By moulding yourself to fit each given situation, you hope the other person won't be angry or upset with you.

In my current relationship, I agreed two rules with my partner – one was that nothing was real until it was said out loud, which included a promise I had made to myself that I wouldn't be the instigator this time. I had always been the person to make the first move on any situation in the past, based on my 'empathic' emotional reading. This time, I decided it was important that I did not try to work off subtext. That meant that, in my mind at least, my partner had to be the one to say it first: he had to be the person who asked me out on a date. This meant that he had to work quite hard to find the words and take the leap, but when he did, I knew it wasn't all a figment of my imagination. The second rule was that neither of us was allowed to grow like an ivy bough and, if we ever suspected that we were, we had to call each other out on it.

The ivy-bough rule doesn't apply only to yourself, however; it also applies to not trying to change the other person. While you might think you can see all the solutions clearly – and know exactly what it is the other person needs to 'fix' – you will end up infantilising them, and eroding their self-esteem and self-belief. If you are one of life's natural fixers, you will need to take a step back from the urge to make all their problems go away or to mould them into something new. Listen without judgement, pop your critical parent voice on pause and support them while they make their own decisions. If those problems appear unsolvable to you, then you need to make a choice. Can you be with this person and love them alongside all of that, or do you need to step back? Remember, what can appear cute in the first rush of love might be extremely irritating three years down the line if you are still living with it. You have to be willing to go the distance with the whole person, not just cherry-pick the parts you like right now with an inward intention of helping them to change the other bits in future. That's just mean. On the flip side, if a day spent with them is better than a day spent without them, then you are probably in the right place.

TRY THIS: WHAT'S IMPORTANT TO YOU (LEVEL TWO)

If you've got this far in your introspection, I congratulate you. This next level might require a little more bravery, but it is helpful if you can stick with it. There are various versions of this next exercise available but here's my pared-down version to get you going.

You will need:

* Your journal and a pen

* Some quiet time to reflect without interruption
* Chocolate, nice music or a soothing location if you feel these will help you

I am going to invite you to create a little inventory of your past relationships. If this feels difficult, take a few deep breaths and imagine what they would look like if they were a movie watched on a rainy Sunday afternoon.

• What would the 'blurb' be for each relationship? How would you summarise the plot of the movie for someone who hadn't seen it?

• What were the circumstances around you? What was going on in your life?

• What was important to you about the person you were in a relationship with?

• What positive traits did they have or bring out in you?

• How did you know they were the right person for you at the time?

• When you split up, what were the circumstances?

• If you think back to your list of ten boundaries, how many of them did this person break?

• What thresholds did you cross? How did you know you had crossed them?

When you have finished this exercise, you will probably have a full and frank exploration of your history. If you were to imagine flying over the situation to get a hawk's eye view of the whole, what is the overriding impression you'd have? What patterns might you notice?

While this might be intensely uncomfortable, know-ing where the bear traps are hidden in the woods will help stand you in very good stead to dodge them in this new relationship.

NAVIGATION: GETTING TO GRIPS WITH OUR EMOTIONS

Just then, Sam passed by and stopped to speak with Elizabeth. He couldn't help but notice her tone was flat and her gaze had turned inward. And so, as if he were waiting for the forest rabbits to emerge from their warren and sit in the sunshine, he patiently waited for her to tell him what troubled her.

He looked thoughtful when she explained, but he did not tell her what she should do and her heart was gladdened. While she was mulling over how to resolve her dilemma, he did not offer words of advice or suggest things she knew would never work, but patiently listened and nodded at her suggestions. Perhaps she could slip back to the tower and retrieve her other paints?

Sam produced an apple and offered it to her for the journey. She smiled and placed it in the pocket of her cloak. It was the first smile she remembered in a long time.

When I met my current partner, a lovely man whom I couldn't have designed better as a 'fit' for me if I had tried, I still had the odd pang of grief for the life I had left behind – those previous relationships (both positive and negative) and even the 'single' status I was hanging up on the coat peg in the porch. Yet while the swampy sadness of those lowland areas can be hard to manage, the highs of finding that perfect faerie glen can be more so. It's time to look at how we gather our emotions at this moment of positive transformation and – witch-like – take control of the situation.

Believe it or not, you are not controlled by your emotions; your emotions are controlled by you. Just let that sink in for a moment.

The thought-feeling-behaviour correlation is actually a sequence that we go through, a sort of chain in which each thing triggers the next. First comes the thought, followed closely by the feeling and then the behaviour in response to the feeling. It all happens in a fraction of a second.

Sometimes, it's easier to identify this chain by working backwards. That behaviour that just occurred – what did you feel in the seconds before you did it? That feeling that you had – what were you thinking in the moments leading up to it? By understanding your emotional patterns and strategies in this way, you can start to consciously isolate the process. And once you get well practised at this, you can begin to change how you feel by paying some attention to your thoughts and which of them are predominant.

There is a process known as metacognition, which describes our ability as humans to be consciously aware of our thought processes and evaluate them. It allows us to step back and assess what we are thinking. It's what Terry Pratchett referred to as 'first thoughts' and 'second thoughts' in his Discworld novels. First thoughts are what you think, while second thoughts are what you think about those thoughts. When we are able to focus in on our second thoughts, we can start to understand the world, ourselves and our reactions a little more fully. As if that's not enough, Pratchett also talks about 'third thoughts' – ones that go off by themselves and take us in a completely new direction. I like to think of second thoughts as happening when we can get in rapport with our unconscious minds and start to direct our lives in a more focused way. They are the inner wisdom that we need to get quiet to hear, to be able to recognise when a piece of wisdom drops in that hasn't come from us alone. Third thoughts are then the wisdom we tap into when we are using a tool like a tarot deck to help us navigate our path. So, how do we open the door to that quality of quietness? Through a little grounding and time spent in nature . . .

TRY THIS: GROUNDING YOURSELF IN NATURE

When you are in the throes of that heady mix of love and confusion, or if you simply want to obtain the peacefulness of communing with your second and third thoughts in any circumstance, take yourself out into your favourite spot in nature, preferably somewhere where you won't be disturbed.

Lay out a groundsheet or blanket and lie down on your back. Take three deep breaths and take a moment to focus on your breath as it passes in and out of your lungs. Feel the steadiness of the earth beneath you, how it rises up to meet your spine, how it supports you. Take another three breaths and focus on what you can see from where you are. Perhaps it is clouds scudding across the sky, or the leaf canopy moving in the breeze. What can you hear? Are there birds singing? The sound of cars far off in the distance? Or is the sound of human traffic much closer? What can you smell? The grass? The earth? The trees? How does the air taste to you? Is it clean and clear, or is there a faint petrol tang? As with our other exercises, you don't need to make a value judgement, just notice what your senses are telling you.

Take another three deep breaths and close your eyes. Listen to the sounds within your body and the sound of your breath going in and out. Notice how your body feels. If you need to shift slightly to get comfortable, you can. What do you notice about your sensory information now? How is it different from when you had your eyes open?

At this point, if you have no other purpose than a little grounding quiet time, keep focusing on your breath for a few more rounds. If you have been pondering a problem or question, take another three deep breaths, open your eyes and focus on a detail in your vision that is moving. Set aside the notion that you have to find a solution to every problem through thinking, and let your awareness move to what your senses can see and hear and touch. Silently ask the earth beneath to support you in locating a solution and see if any impressions rise to the surface. Don't rush it or push it. It is often when we let go of the need to know everything that our third thoughts pop into our awareness. If nothing is coming to the surface right now, know that it will come into your awareness in due course, when you are back in your life, busy preparing a meal or cleaning your bathtub.

ARRIVAL AND DISEMBARKING: QUALITY TIME AND KINDNESS

The next day, the imperfect goddess decided she would return to the tower. She tucked her most treasured possessions in among the branches of the beech tree, knowing that they would come to no harm there. She picked up her walking staff and set off through the trees.

It was further than she remembered on the backward journey. She had, she realised, moved deeper and deeper into the forest, and further and further away from her old life. As she walked each mile, she could feel her old self returning, and it was not altogether a comfortable experience. Her old self sat on her shoulders like an itchy blanket.

As the tower came into sight, Elizabeth gasped. It was in ruins. The roof was cloven in two with scorch marks still visible. The lightning must have struck the tower after she left it that night, a fire ripping through. No wonder her former love had not come looking for her. She must have been given up for lost. The little wooden door was held by only one of its hinges. As she sniffed the air inside, it was stale and unmoving, still stained with the heavy scent of burned wood. There was nothing left for her to retrieve. Nothing would have survived that fire. It was time to close the cover on that time and move on.

With a heart both heavy with grief and freed once more from her old burden, she turned her back on the tower, and made her way back to her forest, and Sam.

As my wise and lovely therapist Shirley has pointed out to me, relationships get more complex as you get older. As life experiences weather the stone of your personalities, and you gather the moss of dependants and other responsibilities, you might start wondering – like me – where you can fit in a new relationship and find the time it takes to create and foster that loving bond with another person. The two pieces of advice I was given by childhood role models who had successful and long-standing relationships were 'Find someone who makes you laugh' (my Umpa) and 'Marry your best friend' (my art teacher at school). When I have questioned more recent role models, they have all concurred, but added one more piece of wisdom: 'Make sure you spend quality time together.'

So, here's the thing: if your life feels like one giant ball of chaos – you might have work, friends, children, animals, study and more work going on – somewhere in all of that you also need to factor in some quality time with your partner. Time when you can step aside from everything else and focus on the two of you and what you both want your relationship to be.

The truth is, relationships might feel like magic, but they are not magical – they need attention and nurturing if they are to take root and grow. You might need to learn a whole new lingo to understand the hobbies and interests of your new love. You might need to build relationships with their children and other loved ones. You might need to start trying things that you haven't tried before (like vegetable gardening or hiking in the mountains), but this is all part of the adventure of setting out on a new quest with a brand-new companion. So while I might have once sneered at the idea of 'date night' – probably because I was so intent on sacrificing myself on the altar of burning love – these days you will find me scheduling them in. I love the opportunity to get away somewhere with my partner and revel in his company, undistracted by phones and emails and demands from other people. I love it when we can go somewhere inspiring and just focus on each other. Thankfully, I really love spending time with him.

MOVING ON: BE KIND

The imperfect goddess returned to her beech tree, her heart saddened by the loss of so much. The birdsong in the trees seemed muted, the colours dimmed by the grief in her heart. But as she walked on, each footstep moving her through the woods, her grief lifted a little. And when she reached her tree, there, resting beneath the branches, writing in his notebook, was Sam waiting to greet her.

Maybe it was the way he listened so carefully to what she told him about her journey, but something in Elizabeth's heart shifted that day and she felt, for the first time, that Sam might be the companion of her heart from now on. Perhaps, she thought, they might look after each other, bonded in common kindness and friendship, and become a family of their own.

When I was learning NLP years ago, there was one ground rule for the training room that stuck, and it's one I think is useful for a new relationship too. 'If you've got a problem, take it to the person who can do something about it.' The idea here is to go to the person you have a problem with – or who might be able to help resolve an issue – rather than spending all your energy talking about it with everyone else in the room. While checking in with your nearest friends can be important for talking things through, there does come a time when you also need to build up that communication bridge with your new partner. This doesn't mean you are trying to change someone – you are asking them to do more of something you like, not alter their whole personality.

No one responds well to being criticised, so it's important to balance the feedback. If you are asking a new partner to do something differently, for example by setting time aside with you to explore your interests as well as theirs, or helping you to remember you can't necessarily fix everything, offer something you really appreciate about them as well. Remember that they have the right and the need to ask you to modify certain things too. If they ask you to do something differently, you don't have to receive it as a personal criticism. It's just feedback – and that's how we learn.

TRY THIS: AN APPLE OF LOVE FOR A NEW RELATIONSHIP

We have various rites of passage for when a couple is ready to make a lasting commitment to each other – for example, marriage ceremonies or what pagans call handfastings. There are fewer, however, for the early stages of a relationship. I am not going to bog you down with the taking of oaths, as it's all too easy to promise things in the first flush of love that then become hard to fulfil and can only lead to disappointment. Instead, let's start with the two of you simply committing to this budding relationship, before seeing if it is what you both want to stick with longer term.

You might say that in the Western creation myths that apples have had an unfairly bad rap (think Adam and Eve and the forbidden fruit), but in other cultures, such as ancient Greek and Norse mythology, the apple was associated with more positive qualities. Apples are not only symbols of love or wisdom in our storytelling traditions, but also in our books of magic. The Grimoires, a source of learning for occult practitioners over the centuries, also associate apples with love and the planet Venus, the pre-modern planetary power connected with all things related to love, friendship, and harmony between people.

In many cultures the apple is a symbol of wisdom and of love, and that is what we are tapping into here. This ritual is designed to be very simple for the two of you to do in private.

You will need:

* An apple
* A sharp knife or a cocktail stick
* Candles to light the room
* An incense of your choosing

Start by washing the apple to ensure that it is clean and any wax or/and preservatives are gone from its surface. Gather with your beloved in a space where you will not be disturbed. Light the candles and the incense to give yourselves a lovely atmosphere. Sit comfortably on some cushions, and place the candles around you, with the incense within easy reach. You should have enough candles so that you can see what you are doing, without causing too much of a fire hazard. Place the apple and the carving implement (the knife or the cocktail stick) between you.

Begin by holding hands and saying:

> We gather on this night,
> In the brightness of new love,
> To signify that I am for you
> And you are for me.

Take up the apple in your left hand and hold it for a moment in the incense smoke to cleanse it (energetically) of anything other than your energy and that of your lover. Pass it to your partner and have them do the same. As you do so, both say:

> We call upon the divine powers of love
> To bless this apple as a symbol of our unity,
> To signify that I am for you
> And you are for me.

Take up the carving implement and carve your lover's initials onto the apple, then have them carve your initials on the other side. As you do so, both say:

> I am for you
> And you are for me.

Now take a bite from the side of the apple where your partner's initials are carved, and pass it to them so they can bite from the side where yours are. Take it in turns to take a bite each, passing it back and forth between you until you reach the core of the apple. If you are an apple core-eater, go right on ahead. If not, place it to one side, and then kiss and say:

> And so it is.

Embrace each other to seal in the magic. Then, if you haven't eaten the apple core, go together and bury it at the foot of a favourite tree or plant.

When you both feel the time is right, you can go full tilt on making vows of commitment to each other in a public or formal setting, but for now enjoy the process of exploring the woods you're in together and getting to know each other. This really is a beautiful time and is to be cherished for as long as you can.

Having wound around the path of early spring in exploring the woodland ways to new relationships, we must now venture deeper into spring, with the fullness of those long-standing big decisions we might make next, like surviving and thriving in our family (whether the one we were born into or one we have chosen), before we begin to explore summer.

CHAPTER FOUR

THE JOURNEY THROUGH SURVIVING AND THRIVING IN YOUR FAMILY

*A wall standing alone is useless, but put three
or four walls together, and they'll support
a roof and keep grain dry and safe.*

*When ink joins with a pen, then the
blank paper can say something.*

*Rushes and reeds must be woven to be useful as a mat. If
they weren't interlaced; the wind would blow them away.*

Jalāl ad-Dīn Muhammad Rūmi

TAROT CARD: The Ten of Cups

'I just want to be normal,' I sobbed. I was eighteen years old and trying hypnotherapy for the first time. I was quite a sickly child – asthma, eczema and multiple allergies – which meant my parents often had to make a midnight dash across the moors to reach the nearest hospital, fifty kilometres away, while I struggled for breath. Each visit to the GP resulted in a hopeful comment that these things tend to go in seven-year cycles, and that maybe I would grow out of it when I reached seven, fourteen, twenty-one ... Of course, I didn't, but that didn't stop me and my mum heading off to every kind of therapy or healing we could find, just in case it would solve the problem.

This was how I found myself lying on a hypnotherapy couch aged eighteen, being regressed to age seven or eight. I distinctly remember standing in the playground of my primary school, crying my little heart out because some boys had been bullying me. With a dad working away, a mum who had to earn a salary in a village with few working mothers, and a home above a hostel for prisoners' visiting families – for which my mum was the warden – I couldn't see anything about my family that was reflected in the experiences of my peers.

The hypnotherapist handled it in the only way a right-thinking, logical person can. 'What is "normal"?' he questioned, and of course the answer that comes to me today is, 'There's no such thing.' Normal is a unicorn, running through the forest, ridden by fairies and trailed by the odd piskie. However, it's likely we have all looked at the family across the road or down the lane and assumed they have it much easier than we do and life in their household must be much nicer than it is in ours.

Family is central to our sense of connection with others and how we feel about ourselves and the world as we grow. It can often feel synonymous with 'home' – a place inseparable from our sense of safety and love and belonging. So it's no wonder that we can feel destabilised and rootless if all is not well with our family.

If we look to archetypes here, they can be quite unhelpful too. For example, the Ten of Cups tarot card, which represents a happy family scenario, often depicts a multi-generational group looking joyous beneath a rainbow or surrounded by ten cups full to the brim. Sometimes it shows an 'average' two-parent family with two children playing happily together nearby. But what happens if that's not familiar to you or if you are not even sure what your birth family was like? How do you begin to build your own family when the original blueprint was dysfunctional or non-existent? And what does family look like today if, like me and my peers, you were brought up with a completely different set of values to the world we live in now? In this chapter, I am going to invite us to think about what family means to each of us, how we can challenge those societal expectations about what a family should look like, and what to do if your family dynamic has more in common with a woodland choked by brambles and poisonous weeds than a tranquil forest glade.

PREPARING FOR THE JOURNEY: THERE'S NO SUCH THING AS NORMAL

Time had moved on, and the imperfect goddess and her man of the greenwood had become as familiar to each other as the constellations in the night sky. She knew the change of sound his breathing made when he drifted into slumber, and he knew her favourite berries and fruits, and the way she nervously tucked her hair behind her ear and twisted its ends when she was thinking hard.

They had begun to gather around them a collection of raggle-taggle birds and creatures of the forest. Once more, Elizabeth had a canine familiar who followed at her heels, though this time it was not a dog, but its vulpine cousin, rich and red and sleek. Its mother had been killed by the hunt that passed far too close for comfort, and Elizabeth had pulled the fox cub to safety in the folds of her cloak as the hounds rushed by. Then there was the cat who had lost a leg, but managed perfectly well on three, and the crow that had become bonded to Sam. They were an odd collection of creatures, human and non-human alike, but they felt a familial bond that transcended their differences.

I hope by now we have established that 'normal' is not only a mythical beast, but it also can be quite a harmful label to try to live up to. The wonderful thing about reaching adulthood is that you have a little more autonomy to organise your life and your family units in the way that *you* choose. While we all have a set of cards that life has dealt us, we can also reshuffle them a little or ask the dealer for a substitute or two. Things now look quite different from the 'norms' of each of our childhoods.

In nature, the family unit is just as diverse as it is in the human world, but it does give us an indication of how important a strong family unit can be. They are by no means always 'one-male-one-female' in their make-up, however. Elephants form a strong bond within their herd, which can number anywhere between eight and one hundred elephants, all led by one matriarch – the wise one of the group who holds the memories about where to find food and water. But the strong matriarchal nature of the herd means that it has little use for the males, who tend to leave at puberty, just as they are entering into the spring of their lives, and forge a path for themselves elsewhere. Orcas, too, see raising offspring as a group activity, with multiple members of the pod working together to protect and teach their young. Food is shared within the family unit, ensuring that nobody goes without. In the bird world, and specifically in the buzzard family, the male and female build the nest together, but the maternal, nurturing instincts reside with the female; she does most of the work in incubating the brood of eggs they produce, while the male brings home the food. When the eggs hatch, the emphasis is all on fast learning, as the buzzard chicks have to discover how to survive in the world as quickly as possible. With almost three-quarters of buzzards dying of starvation before they reach maturity at age three, it is imperative they learn to hunt and catch food as quickly as they can, before they are turfed out of the nest in the summertime to fend for themselves.

What we see if we survey the natural world is a diverse range of family units, each of which has its strong points and its hindrances, that are largely designed to rear young and equip them with what they need to survive in the outside world, but also – in the case of animals that live in herds – groups that continue to offer care and advice, which we will come back to in later chapters. The point is, there is no 'one size fits all'.

So, let's reframe that question: 'What is normal?' Perhaps what we are really asking is related to how a family functions, and whether it is healthy. It may be easy to describe a dysfunctional family, but if you were to picture a functional and happy family enjoying a summer outing in nature together, what would it look like? The obvious assumption is that it involves two parents of opposite genders, although that is increasingly no longer the case. In 2020, there were 2.9 million lone-parent families in the UK, which accounts for 14.7 per cent of all families. Homes containing multiple families are the fastest-growing type of household over the last two decades – just as with sea otters and prairie dogs, who all gather in large groups of families, sharing of resources can be the best way to survive and thrive. Other changes are at play too – nearly two decades on from the Adoption and Children Act, which in 2005 gave LGBTQIA+ families the right to adopt, and the jump forwards in medical techniques that allowed IVF to be a viable option for conception, record numbers of families are no longer limited to notions of the traditional one-man-one-woman model. Diverse families can (and definitely do) provide loving and enriching family environments for children of any gender, just like our animal cousins.

When we turn our attention to why things might go wrong in people's lives, as reflected in our wider communities, it is also helpful to touch on the causes of societal breakdown that can be linked to a malfunctioning family unit. When it comes to the cause of crime- or addiction-related issues, the work of Gabor Maté, the renowned Canadian doctor and addiction expert, points the way to early childhood trauma as the trigger. In spite of popular political rhetoric, it is not down to one-parent or indeed multiple-parent set-ups, but to whether or not our developmental needs are met during these crucial developmental periods of childhood: the most essential component for healthy development is a child's relationship with their caring adults. It's not rocket science, but it's surprising how many of us are unaware of these links. As the ancient Chinese philosopher Lao Tzu wrote in the *Tao Te Ching*, way back in 400 BCE:

> Thirty spokes are joined together in a wheel,
> But it is the centre hole
> That allows the wheel to function.
> We mould clay into a pot,
> But it is the emptiness inside
> That makes the vessel useful.
> We fashion wood for a house,
> But it is the emptiness inside
> That makes it liveable.
> We work with the substantial,
> But the emptiness is what we use.

So if we are to use the Tao analogy for a functional family, perhaps it is one that allows space for each individual member to be nurtured and supported to grow, whether they are an adult or a child. We all need supportive spaces where we can explore and learn about life, allowing us to strengthen ourselves through the spring and summer of our lives, in order that, when the winter months come creeping back in, we are better able to cope.

Psychology Today defines the functional family as one in which:

> Parents strive to create an environment in which everyone feels safe and respected. A positive home requires parents to set and uphold rules, but not resort to overly rigid regulation of any one person's behaviour. In a healthy

household, slights and misbehaviours are readily addressed, and boundaries are clear and consistent, all of which help avoid disharmony in the longer term.

For me, there are obvious parallels between this description and the Wiccan coven. Like the elephant herds, Wiccan groups favour the matriarchal set-up, with the male element varying from supportive role to supportive-equal, depending on the individual make-up of the leadership. Covens are a gathering of like-minded individuals who over time come together in a close-knit group that is intended to create a nourishing base from which to live your life. Group dynamics are crucial here, though: if the group is to remain healthy and flourish, everyone needs to be working towards the same end point – a sunny woodland glade in which they can all flourish – or we will start to see those unhealthy family dynamics creeping across the ground again.

While many people crave the status of high priest or high priestess, it's hard work, and requires careful thought to keep that dynamic well and functioning – and this, of course, is true for biological families too. Creating healthy groups of people in real life is a complex business and requires careful cultivation. For example, bad weather and conflict are natural parts of human life, and have to exist in order for us to be able to explore our boundaries. However, if you have grown up in a family where all the conflict happened behind closed doors, and there were no reasonable adult conversations, this can make the mildest of discussions feel frightening and uncontained. You can end up catastrophising over every-day, healthy conflict.

The only way to work through these blueprint limitations is to practise, hopefully within a family unit with whom you can be honest and who can be honest with you. The trick is to allow 'conflicts' to be explored in a measured way, so that both adults and children feel equally safe. Disagreements or angry feelings can be talked through without shouting or slamming doors. It's less about nature versus nurture – the key concept is really that all of us are saplings, whatever our nature, and we require support in order to grow.

TRY THIS: AN AIR-CLEARING INCENSE

There are times when our homes can feel a little like a tangled wood. Discord is inevitable from time to time – in fact, suppressing a lack of agreement is not a healthy thing to do. Sometimes it's better to clear the air, however difficult it feels. If you have cleared the air but now feel the need to literally clear the air, I invite you to join me in a little session of saining.

Saining is a traditional Scottish folk-magic ritual, very similar to Native American smudging. Those involved would close all the doors and windows, bank up the fire and then throw herbs on the fire to cause it to smoke. Traditionally, this would have been juniper. When the house was filled with smoke in every corner, the doors and windows would be thrown open, allowing the smoke to escape, taking with it any negative influences, either from spirits or from people.

In this version of the ritual, we are going to create a loose incense to clear the air and bring a little harmony back into your home. For instructions as to how to burn a loose incense, please refer back to Chapter One. It is a good idea to keep any children or non-humans away from the incense smoke.

You will need:

* Half a teaspoon of dried juniper (about four berries)
* A dessertspoon of frankincense pearls
* Half a teaspoon of dried sage leaves crushed up into small pieces

* Six drops of rose essential oil
* A pinch of cinnamon
* A charcoal disc and censer, prepared as described on pages 23–4

Begin by grinding the juniper berries into small pieces in a pestle and mortar, then add the frankincense pearls and the sage, and grind them too. Finally add the essential oil and the cinnamon.

When your charcoal disc has been lit and is ready, add a small pinch of the incense to the heated disc. Carry the censer around the house, visiting every room to ensure the smoke reaches all the corners. When you are ready, open the windows and let the fresh air blow through. Invite your family – whatever that looks like to you – back in to enjoy the calm and cleansed space together.

CHARTING YOUR COURSE: BEING CHILDLESS OR CHILD-FREE

The imperfect goddess sometimes wondered if she and her wood man would have children of her own. Yet each month as the moon passed its fullness, she continued to bleed. Sometimes at night she stayed awake and gazed up through the leaf canopy into the face of the moon and asked what they might do in order for a child to come. But the moon stayed petulant and full, keeping her secrets hidden on the other side.

Elizabeth buried her face in the hair of the woodsman, and felt the warmth of the little fox as she curled up by her feet. Over time, she resolved to be happy and embrace the family she already had.

One of the potential directions that comes up in our journey around this part of the woods is the pathway towards children. This is an area where not everyone gets to choose. Fecund springtime doesn't come for all of us. For some, childlessness or the inability to have as many children as we'd hoped is the source of immense pain; even with IVF, failure rates are high. For others, it may be that the right economic, romantic, housing or familial circumstances haven't come into play – and then, somehow, time passes and you realise it's no longer physically possible. Others – around 10 per cent of women in the UK – make an active choice to be child-free, preferring instead to focus on other experiences in their lives, their work or the richness of their life as it is; sometimes the choice is made because of concerns about the effects of climate change on the next generation, or the state of the world when we pass it on, but this is not a new phenomenon. According to the *New York Times* in an article entitled 'Why Women Not Having Kids Became a Panic', women have made this choice through history, particularly in times of economic uncertainty, like the Depression of the 1920s, or among groups who live further away from their familial support networks or in ways that don't conform to society's expectations.

Gateway Women is a network for childless women that works to raise awareness of some of the issues facing women who are involuntarily childless. Its founder, Jody Day, an inspirational TEDx speaker, notes that talking about childlessness is still a taboo: the grief of something that never existed so often goes unnoticed. How can you grieve for a child you have never had?

TRY THIS: GRIEVING FOR A CHILD YOU NEVER HAD

This is a ritual you can perform alone, to give yourself space to grieve and let go of the child you didn't have. You may never have been pregnant, or a pregnancy may have ended through choice or through miscarriage: whatever the circumstances, you have lost the future you might have had with a child (or children), both in terms of the personalities they may have had, and in yourself. You would have been different if you had fulfilled the ambition of becoming a parent. By marking the loss with a ritual, the hope is that you can release the grief in order to be able to integrate the experience into your life.

I've participated in ceremonies where a paper boat was created and a tea light was placed in it and sent out to sea, and while those ideas are lovely, we don't want to pollute the natural world with soggy bits of paper and metal tea-light cases, or risk harming wildlife in the process. Instead we are going to focus on using the ingredients the natural world can give us. I once performed this ceremony for a friend I had lost, so it can be adapted to any grieving situation.

You will need:

* A pen
* Some green leaves of spring

Take yourself out to a quiet spot near a water source. A river or a stream is ideal, or the sea if you live near it, especially if you visit with the ebbing tide (i.e. when the tide is going out). As you travel to the magical spot you have chosen, select a green leaf for each child or each aspect of the lost dream of parenthood that you need to let go of or mark. Focus on the beauty of the natural world around you as you walk. Even if you are in a town, there will be plenty of trees, animal or bird life around you. Notice the way that nature will often flow into the void left by a loss and fill all the spaces that are left.

When you reach your water source, sit or stand for a moment and focus on your leaves. Use the pen to write the name of the lost child (or the lost potential) onto the leaf. Focus on the love that you feel for that child – even if they never made it into physical life, that doesn't mean you can't send them some love now. If you can step into the water source, do, as it can sometimes help to physicalise the symbolism of the ritual. If you're close to the river, face downstream; if you are at the sea, it is the tidal pull that will carry your grief away.

Say the following words out loud, or quietly in your head if it feels more fitting:

> Child of mine, whether you were here in life with me or in my dreams of a life with you, I love you. For the life I have here and now, and in hopes that we may meet one day in other circumstances, I release you with love.

Let each leaf go into the current of the water, and watch as it floats away from you.

The reality of childlessness is that it leaves people with a different kind of empty space, in which go all the experiences they yearned for: milestone birthday parties, first days at school, school plays and endless trips to the park. They will never get to experience being the mother of their partner's child, to see how that child would have looked, who they would have become. Even if remaining child-free was an active decision, it doesn't mean you won't feel grief or regret for the life you never quite had.

That's not to say that having children is plain sailing either, particularly for those facing single parenthood in a workplace not designed to mesh with the school calendar, or for parents bringing up children without the support of extended family. Changes in our economy mean that one of you being a 'stay at home' parent is now much more often a decision born of privilege than the common set-up it once was. Even if we actively enjoy the career-building possibilities this facilitates, it's hard to imagine those non-working mothers in my childhood village still existing today.

It's clear that family units are changing and evolving. Today a 'family' may consist of a childless couple and their cat, or a partnership that meets later in life and that blends their family units together, including children from a former relationship. We all have the freedom to decide what family looks like for us, even if it doesn't resemble the Waltons (who'd want it to?) or our own imagined ideal. So, let's start unpicking the choices that exist for you.

EMBARKING ON THE JOURNEY: CREATING YOUR OWN FAMILY

One morning, as the imperfect goddess and her man of the greenwood were down by the river fishing for rainbow trout, Elizabeth had a vague awareness they were being watched. Her senses prickled with the feeling that another pair of eyes was upon her, but when she glanced up there was no one there.

She asked Sam about who lived there in the forest with them.

'There are stories,' he told her, 'of the wild god who lives among the trees. The people of the village tell their children to stay out of the woods, especially after dark.'

Elizabeth wondered if it was just her and Sam that were being mistaken for a wild god, but she couldn't help being intrigued. Who was the god, and was he as frightening as people said? She thought back to her encounter with Death, and how people had thought he was frightening too. Yet up close he was gentle, not harsh, and loving, not foreboding. She shrugged off her disquietude, determined not to believe the stories. She would make up her own mind once she had encountered the wild god for herself.

Over the coming weeks, each time Elizabeth wandered forest paths filled with hawthorn blossom, wild cherry and cow parsley, she knew that something watched, something was waiting for her among the trees. When she swam in the warming river, when she gathered dandelions and nettles, she knew it was there. Yet, she could not catch a glimpse.

As a teenager, I was lucky enough to be introduced by my sister to the *Tales of the City* novels by Armistead Maupin. They were originally written as newspaper columns centring on a young man, Michael 'Mouse' Tolliver, living in San Francisco in the 1970s. At the heart of these tales was Number 28 Barbary Lane, owned by Anna Madrigal, a dope-smoking libertarian who gathered in all the waifs and strays who crossed her path. Each had their own story, and their own set of circumstances that had led them to seek a new life in the city. For Mouse, his search sits against the backdrop of coming to terms with his family's rejection of his sexuality.

The reason I mention Maupin's marvellous *Tales* is that he introduced me to the idea of having a biological family (the family you are born into that you cannot choose) and a logical family (the family you can gather around you purely by choice). Wiccan covens are logical families, as the members of a group undergo a gradual process of selection and integration over a longish period. Just because someone says they want to join a coven doesn't mean they will make it through.

Wicca is also a religion that centres on ancestor veneration. We actively invite our ancestors into every witches' circle or gathering and some festivals are completely focused on this aspect. For example, at Samhain each autumn, we take time to reconnect to our departed loved ones. Students often ask me, 'What do I do if I don't know who my ancestors are?' or 'What do I do if my ancestors were despicable people who did terrible things?' My answer is always to direct them to another kind of ancestor – the logical ones.

TRY THIS: JOURNALING A LIST OF YOUR LOGICAL FAMILY

Sometimes we need to make the unconscious conscious, and it can help to write a list of your logical family and ancestors in your notebook or journal. So, I invite you to sit for a moment and do just that.

When thinking of your logical family members, you might choose to centre on friends that you have chosen to fill your life with. You might want to include your partner's friends or family too, if you have been adopted into another family, whether officially or in spirit.

When considering your ancestors, who inspires you? Whose footsteps are you walking in as you make your way through the woods? Who were your mentors? If someone has paved the way for you, then you can claim them as your logical ancestor – you don't have to have met them in person. For example, I would consider the esoteric writers Sylvia Townsend Warner (who wrote about witchcraft, among many other things) and Mary Webb (the nature mystic) as my logical ancestors, both of them ploughing individual and original furrows.

The key function of family is to foster your sense of safety, love, belonging and connection. Yet if you have been born into a family where this kind of care and appreciation was absent, or if you have found yourself estranged from your biological family, don't give up entirely on the concept. Your chosen, logical family also extends to the people who have nurtured you and helped you to grow in myriad ways. If you were adopted as a child, and you never knew your birth family, or if you have found yourself in the privileged and sometimes complex situation of becoming a step-parent later in life, or if you decide to foster or adopt, there are infinite ways in which you can nurture the seedlings or saplings of a chosen family.

As Mouse demonstrates amply in *Tales of the City*, you can create the family you always wanted to have, from the friends who are closest to you and the connections you choose to build.

NAVIGATION: THE STORIES WE TELL

Gradually, over time, Elizabeth learned to be more cunning while she watched for the wild god to show himself. Each time she sensed him moving between the trees, she would keep her head still but allow her eyes to dart to one side. And so it continued, until the wild god grew bolder and was ready to be seen.

The wild god, it seemed, wasn't a scary beast at all. There peering at her from behind a tree was a small boy – his hair all matted and filled with twigs, his face grimy and tear-streaked. Each time she turned to smile at him, he darted away between the layers of the forest. Yet each time he returned, he came a little closer. When the imperfect goddess held out her hand and offered the ripe red apple she had plucked that morning to the trees, the boy looked at it, licked his lips and hesitated. She held it out again and smiled and this time, to her great delight, he edged towards her, reached out a grubby hand and took the apple, eating it hungrily.

'My name is Elizabeth,' she told the small wild god, hoping he might respond in kind.

'Do you remember that time you came running into the living room on Christmas Day, with your skirt hitched up in your knickers and a piece of toilet roll trailing out behind?'

Most of us, at one time or another, have been at one of those family gatherings where people start sharing stories and memories. Often, it's when you've brought a new partner home to meet the family and all your most embarrassing moments start worming their way out. Or it's at a wedding, where apparently hundreds of people get to witness your discomfort. Then one day you realise that your memory of an event is completely different from that of your Aunty Joan or Uncle Philip, who keep on telling the story, even while the 'truth' of it is questionable. As the expert in communication Danielle McGeough writes: 'Family storytelling is a complex process that creates and disrupts understandings.' Each retelling brings with it a little more embellishment – a detail here, a tweak there – until the oft-told tale bears little resemblance to the original event. McGeough puts this down to the fragmentary approach to family storytelling:

> A family may operate as though its members share mutual understandings even when this is not the case, completely unaware that they have different versions of stories. Other times, differences are neglected in order to maintain cohesion among family members, and even when versions of stories are 'corrected', the influence of the original story remains.

It's perfectly natural for humans to delete, distort and misremember stories – our unconscious is designed this way, because we can't possibly remember every detail of every encounter. Even if you can recount an event word for word as you remember it, this is your *perception* of the event and each person has their own unique version. It doesn't make one 'righter' than another. I once had a huge row with someone who was adamant that their version of a memory was 'true' and 'right'. They just couldn't get their head around the idea that another version, equally as valid, could exist.

You can probably see where I am going with this one. The problem with collective story-telling is when it becomes rigid, leaving family members stuck in outmoded and out-of-date stories that simply may no longer be true. For example, there is an old story of how bad-tempered I was as a child. One day, I was misbehaving at the dinner table and, out of frustration, my mother put me in a 'time out' in my room. The trouble was I was too short to reach the door handle, which obviously I wanted to use to escape, so spent the next few minutes stamping round the room, shouting at the top of my lungs. All of this earned me the nickname of Rumpelstiltskin. The problem with this is that I must have been very small (the door handles weren't that high) and although I haven't had a full-blown temper tantrum for decades, that story – and its associations – stuck. In my family I was the angry child, my sister was the good girl and my brother the naughty one who was always getting into trouble, and so go all the tales we tell about each other.

Conversely, this labelling of family members and the resultant storytelling are all about bonding a group and ensuring that each family member understands their role. So is it any surprise that if you come from a family of multiple siblings, you will each have grown up in an apparently different family? The roles we play differ according to where we are in the line-up (youngest, middle, eldest or solo), and the relationships we have with our parents will differ too, even when parents make a concerted effort to treat each child equally. Yet there is a difference between equality (all being treated the same) and equity (all being given what you need in order to get a fair footing). However universal you think the experiences were in your family, they're not.

If we allow these labels and these stories to perpetuate into adulthood, they can become destructive and belittling, stunting our growth and sense of self.

This is where positive reframing can become your friend. Every time Uncle Geoffrey says, 'Remember that time you had a tantrum? Oh, you were such a little firecracker,' you can simply smile, and reply, 'Thank you! I've always appreciated my sparkiness.' Each time that story about 'how boring' you've always been raises its head, you reply, 'Thank you. I've always been proud of my steady approach to life.' And for every accusation of being 'over-sensitive,' you reply, 'Thanks. I've always been proud of my sensitivity – it's such a useful life skill.'

Get the idea? You can even prepare your responses in advance if you know exactly what will come up next time you have a family dinner. Just think of all the stories that are told about you and get ready for some positive reframing. It's great for seeing the expression on someone's face change in front of your eyes . . . especially if you can add a new and more recent tale to the mix that allows for a sense of surprise and for them to see you anew.

A word of caution, however. If you don't like the stories your family tells about you, you also need to be aware of the tales you tell about them. It's not a fair trade if you object to what they remember but perpetuate well-trodden myths about them too. Sometimes in life we must model good behaviour to elicit change in those we love.

TRY THIS: UNDERSTANDING THE LABELS WE USE AND WHAT THEY MEAN

For this exercise, I am going to invite you, once more, to spend some time with your journal. Take yourself off to a quiet space where you won't be disturbed and take your notebook and pen.

Begin by asking yourself, 'What is important to me about "family"?' Pay attention to the words you identify. What are their associations?

If the words you have identified represent quite abstract concepts (as with me and my sense of what was 'normal'), you might find that making those concepts more sensory and rooted in a physical experience helps you get to grips with what is important.

For example, 'normal' to me might have meant not sticking out like a sore thumb among my peers, or it might have sounded like children playing happily, instead of being bullied. You can also substitute the word 'normal' here for whatever emotive hot words come up for you. The word 'happy', for example, can often be a bit of a trigger if you imagine that everyone else's family was completely content, while yours didn't feel that way.

> What does [normal] look like?
> What does [normal] feel like?
> What does [normal] taste like?
> What does [normal] smell like?
> What does [normal] sound like?
> How will you know when you have achieved [normal]? What will you be doing specifically, when you realise you have achieved [normal]?

For example, 'happy' might taste like your favourite dinner with your family, or it might smell like a hot bath with lavender oil. If you have managed to create a fully formed sensory picture of that label in your journal, consider the following two additional questions:

> Where in your life do those sensory experiences manifest? (I.e., if you aren't feeling normal, what is the closest you get?)

If you have failed to quantify what that term feels like physically, or if you have created a sensory picture that isn't as compelling as you thought it might be, can you acknowledge that the label might not be all that you had imagined it would be, and now let it go?

MOVING ON: BECOMING A WHY CHILD AGAIN

'My name is Robin Goodfellow,' the small boy said, 'but my mother used to call me Puck.' Elizabeth shivered when she heard his voice, as it carried with it the weight of a thousand stories, in spite of his quiet tone.

'Then I shall call you that too,' the imperfect goddess said decisively.

Puck came home with Elizabeth that day, and met Sam and vixen and the other animals that had decided to make up their woodland family. Puck was an orphan and had come to live in the forest when the people of his village had turned aside from him. Elizabeth started to enjoy her daily walks with Puck. When he had forgotten that he needed to be shy, his curiosity bounded ahead of them. Each spring flower they passed had to be named for him – violet, primrose, celandine – and each bird identified – black cap, goldfinch, chiffchaff – and listed in turn. Elizabeth found herself learning her world all over again through the eyes of the small wild god who had chosen her and Sam as his family.

I've spent a lot of time between the covers of various self-help and spiritual development books over the years, but where many fall down is that they can encourage you to solve the symptoms of a problem, without giving due attention to the deep-rooted structural cause.

In my working life, I often assist with incident investigations, carrying out risk assessments to identify the underlying issue, with the simple idea that if you find out why something has happened, you are more likely to be able to stop it from happening again in the future. Now, please don't misunderstand me. This is not one of those books that will imply, or even inform you, that all of your problems have come for a reason. I don't believe that we invite serious illness or death in, however unconsciously. On the other hand, there are changes you can be determined to make in your life if you start to identify why you have gone down a particular path in the first place. While you might think of incidents as things that happen at work, in our family lives there can also be occurrences that we need to get to the bottom of, not least to return us to a sense of a calm, peaceful forest, instead of a bramble-choked glade. This is to help you identify and remove those potentially poisonous weeds.

When I train incident investigators, I give them an exercise called 'The Whys', using the example of an unhappy client coming into an addiction treatment service and behaving very aggressively. If I ask a team member why the incident took place, they will sometimes tell me that it occurred 'because the person was aggressive', at which point I again ask, 'Why?' Why was the person aggressive? Then we start to get somewhere, with a reason that is closer to the root cause. 'The person was aggressive as they had been kept waiting for their appointment, and they hadn't been told how long the wait would be.' Again, why? 'They weren't told why they had to wait as we were dealing with a medical emergency in one of the other rooms.' Now we're really rolling. What would you do differently if this came up again in future? Make sure the receptionist apologised for the wait and explained that the staff were helping someone who was very unwell.

To give you a more common 'real-life' example, imagine you've had a disagreement with someone in your family. You've become angry, but they don't feel it warranted such a strong response and that you've overreacted. When you first ask yourself why you became angry, your answer might be, 'Because they annoyed me.' Is that something you can change? No, you can't control other people, you can only control how you respond to them, so we need to dig a little deeper. Why did they annoy you? 'Because they assumed they knew what I wanted and needed and told me so.' Is that the root cause? Can you change this? No, so, again, let's go further. Why did this specifically trigger your anger? 'Because my ex-partner always used to make decisions about things without asking me what I wanted, which made me feel completely powerless and invisible.'

Ah. This to me feels like the root cause, that underlying structural reason for your response. At this point you can choose to explain to the family member why you reacted as you did. It might make you feel strange at first, and you may need to choose how much you're happy to reveal, but adults tend to respond better if you can take some responsibility for how you behaved and will feel closer to you if you can trust them with where this has come from. We are all human and can't always get it right all the time.

TRY THIS: A RITUAL FOR FORMING A CHOSEN FAMILY

In many cultures, the dinner table is seen as the heart of the family unit. In my family, whatever we were doing, we sat together to eat dinner each evening, and I still have warm memories of the conversations and activities undertaken around that old oak table.

In some religions, there are traditional meals and foods eaten as part of a specific family festival. In witches' circles, we end every ritual with a shared meal – each bringing a dish to eat with the rest of the coven or family group. In the West, the Christmas lunch often performs a similar function – we gather at a prescribed time and share a set menu of family favourite dishes. Is yours a prawn-cocktail-starter kind of group or a straight-to-the-turkey family? On Pesach, Jewish families gather around the Seder, a ritual plate containing seven foods, which represent the story of the Jewish people being set free from slavery in Egypt at Passover. In the Zoroastrian faith, the New Year is celebrated by sharing the seven foods of the Haft-seen, where each food is symbolic of nature, which is central to the Haft-seen celebration. See where I am heading? Sevens are significant in many world faiths, and it's the number that most people are likely to pick as their favourite. With seven oceans in the world, seven days of the week, seven colours in the rainbow, seven continents, seven classical planets and so on, it's also very familiar, ingrained as a number in our everyday. In numerology, the number seven represents logic, understanding, spirituality and intellect, the search for deeper meaning. In pre-modern planetary magic, it is also the number of the planet Venus, representing love and friendship, so we are going to make use of the spiritual seven in our ritual today.

I would invite you to gather your family – be it logical or biological – for a ritual to celebrate your bond and the inception or confirmation of this supportive group. If you have a favourite family meal, this is the time to prepare it, whether it's a roast, a chilli, a curry or whatever food of fond memories and connection. It's important too that this meal is eaten at a family table. If, like many of us, you live in a small space without the luxury of a dining room or large kitchen, you might need to get creative. Perhaps you could gather at a picnic site with an outdoor table? If you are in nature, you are already in sacred space.

If you are indoors, clean the space, air it well and focus on creating a loving atmosphere – gentle music in the background, the table set with a cloth and candles, each person seated at an equal height. Gather everyone around to help set the table. Include a plant or a vase of flowers to remind everyone (even if unconsciously) that nature is a part of everything we do. We want equality and equity here. If you are outdoors, you could improvise with homemade storm lanterns – tea lights in jam jars. While this is happening, you will also need to prepare the following dishes in addition to the main meal. Feel free to substitute any of them if you have a better idea for a symbolic food that means something to your family:

1. A loaf of bread for the safety and security you will foster for each other
2. A dish of salt water for the cleansing tears you sometimes shed together
3. A dish of milk (it can be vegan) to symbolise nourishment
4. A dish of honey to represent kind words
5. An apple cut across its equator into rings, so you can see the Venusian star at the centre. This represents the love that binds you as a family. You want one slice per person, so you may need more than one apple.
6. Chocolate for the sweetness and comfort of the family unit
7. Wine (or grape juice) for the many times you will celebrate each other's successes

Gather the family around the table and light the candles. If holding hands around the group feels just too much, then don't – otherwise join hands and have one person say the following out loud:

> On this day [state the day and date] we, the newly formed [insert your chosen family name] family gather together to pledge our bonds with each

other. From here onwards, we will be each other's solace, safety and springboard. We will provide the security of love and kindness and nurturing. When one of us struggles, we will all gather round and form a protective circle. Here, we pledge our vow to each other.

The first person then tears off a hunk of bread and says:

The bread represents the safety and security we will create for each other.

Pass the loaf to the next person in a clockwise direction. Each person should then take a piece of bread and echo the words of the first person.

Next, take the dish of salt water. Dip a little of the bread in it and say:

The salt water represents the tears we sometimes shed together.

Eat the bread, then pass the dish to the person on your right and allow them to do the same. When everyone has done this, take the dish of milk. Dip a little of the bread in the milk and say:

The milk represents the ways in which our family will nourish each other.

Eat the milky bread and pass the dish round as before.

Continue with the dish of honey. Dip a little of the bread it and say:

> The honey represents our kind words for each other.

Eat the honeyed bread and pass the dish round. Next take a slice of the apple and say:

> The apple represents the love that binds us.

Eat the apple, pass the dish round, then take a piece of the chocolate and say:

> The chocolate represents the sweetness and comfort of our family.

Eat the piece of chocolate and pass the dish round. Finally, take the cup of wine or grape juice, take a sip and say:

> I drink a toast to us. While life may have taken us in directions we were not expecting, and we may sometimes feel lost and afraid, I promise to try to be there for each of you when you need me.

When each of you has given the toast, join hands again if you feel able. As you say the next few words, make sure to make eye contact with each person around the table.

> Blessed be this place, this time and they who are with us.

When you have finished the ritual, you can share the main dinner and ensure that each person at the table is heard in what they want to share.

Families can be the source of great discomfort and anguish, but they can also be the source of great support and safety. You have a choice to make together, and I hope that this ritual enables you to pledge something of that intention to each other.

Hopefully by now you are gathered in a home that enables you to grow and develop, with people around you who nurture and support you. It is time to move on into the woods of early summer, to explore how your life might be changing further from here on. Perhaps you are starting to feel that it is time for you to turn your attention to your own self-fulfilment, and think about where you find your joys, how you find your flow and even (gulp) how you might move your life geographically to a home that will further support your quest for more peaceful perambulations around the woods.

PART THREE
SUMMER IN THE WOODS

Face to face with the sunflower,
Cheek to cheek with the rose,
We follow a secret highway
Hardly a traveller knows.
The gold that lies in the folded bloom
Is all our wealth;
We eat of the heart of the forest
With innocent stealth.

Mary Webb

THEMES: Sovereignty, courage
PLANET: Sun
ELEMENT: Fire
DIRECTION: South
TIME OF DAY: Midday

In summer, the woods simmer gently, a heated haze hanging between the trees as the day reaches its zenith. I arrive as early as I can in search of the quiet stillness of early morning. The leaves are now fully matured and the bracken stands high, clothing me in green to the waist. Down at the river in early morning, the shallow water is covered in pond skaters, their spindly legs moving with speed across the surface, barely breaking through. The dippers fly upstream, a brown and white streak of energy, broadcasting a high-pitched song as they zip above the surface of the water. Later in the day this space will become busy with people, all seeking the cool flow. The ponies will continue to amble through the spaces of the valley, unconcerned by the sudden influx, despite the teenage boys running and leaping into the water of my favourite pool, leaving me to seek out quieter places further upstream.

By summer, the hawthorn petals have fallen, its former flower heads forming tight green berries, which will mature through the summer months. In one small batch of Devon banking, a spread of tiny wild strawberries has emerged in among the green. I stop and nibble at a few of them – as sweet and luscious as their larger cousins, although minute in scale. A sudden breeze releases a cloud of dandelion seeds, white feathers blowing upwards towards the sun. In planetary magic, the dandelion holds a unique place – its flower heads classified as being under the dominion of the sun; its white clock heads ruled by the moon.

This morning, at the edge of the pool, a discarded dragonfly larva's exoskeleton has been left clinging to a tree root, its translucent shell-like quality miraculous in its survival. The dragonflies, meanwhile, freed of their former confines, dart above the river – the electric blue and green of the banded demoiselle, the black and yellow of the southern hawker. They will typically live for only a week or two, their lives so fleeting, but a reminder for us to savour each breath of this fecund moment before the turn towards autumn.

Summer brings the height of all that we associate with positivity and light – the days at their longest, a sense of limitless possibility in the air. And so, the life changes we will visit in the next two chapters are themed around sovereignty and courage: finding your flow and finding a sense of home and belonging in these soft, languid days.

CHAPTER FIVE

THE JOURNEY TOWARDS FINDING YOUR FLOW OR YOUR PERFECT CAREER

Here lies one whose name was writ in water

From the gravestone of John Keats

TAROT CARD: The Fool, the Six of Pentacles, the Wheel of Fortune or the Ace of Pentacles

'What do you want to be when you grow up?' seems to be a question many Western societies are obsessed with asking children from a fairly young age. Yet some of us ask this same question of ourselves as we continue through life. It can sometimes feel that, unless you have decided on your career path by the age of eight and 'made it' by your teen years, you must be a colossal failure. I have worked with students who honestly feel that they have to reach the pinnacle of success by the time they are thirty or they may as well go home and build a blanket fort to live in. One of the many things wrong with this model is that it is based on a handful of 'true-life stories' from people who have become wildly successful at a very early age. We love a tale of overnight success, but when you look more closely at the details, the reality is usually a lot more complex. If I had gone with the original idea of what I wanted to be as a child, I would have gone to the New York High School of Performing Arts, and you would certainly not be reading this book now. (To date, I haven't been to New York, let alone become one of the 'Kids from Fame'. I don't even like musicals these days.)

And what about those of us who have had to 'settle' for a job or a career path in order to survive? One that perhaps doesn't set our world alight every morning, but where that regular monthly salary pays the rent or mortgage, and all those other bills that keep coming in. Where does inspiration, or our dream of an inspired life, fit in with the day-to-day task of 'adulting'? If we can't fulfil our dreams of a fabulous fantasy existence, how do we bring more of our passion into the everyday?

Our lives develop and grow like woodland trees – sometimes branching off in unexpected directions, leafing, flowering and fruit-ing at moments of growth and change, but also entering a time of wintering or stasis. We aren't meant to be constantly on the 'up'. The truth is that there is more to you than how you earn a living, and how you choose to do that may change over time as other areas of your life develop alongside.

In this chapter, we will explore (and perhaps explode) some commonly held misconceptions about the world of work and careers, and how this fits (or doesn't) with your sense of flow – that chimerical state where you find that you lose all sense of time and space, as you wrap yourself up in the thing that you love. How can you weave that into your daily living (if at all) and how does it con-tribute to that elusive sense of purpose; what can you expect when seeking success; and how can you set out on a new path through the woods when you have already spent twenty years plodding in a very different direction? In short, how do you fill your days with the things you love most, while still earning a living?

Spoiler alert. There are no easy answers in this chapter, but I always think it's better to have a sense of the true lie of the land rather than being told you are strolling to the beach before finding out you must schlep up a mountain first. After all, it might be from the top of that hard-won peak that the lie of the land finally becomes clear.

Along the way, I'll introduce you to some activities to help you to find your flow through the dizzying array of possibilities that you *could* embrace when you grow up. Even if, like me, you were officially grown up a long time ago.

PREPARING FOR THE JOURNEY: HOW TO BE AN OVERNIGHT SUCCESS (OR ACHIEVING MASTERY VERSUS FINDING YOUR FLOW)

While the imperfect goddess was gathering a woodland family all around her, she still felt there was one aspect of her desires that she had not yet managed to fulfil –her own craftmanship. While spending time with her man of the woods and the little wild god gave her a sense of belonging and of family, she still wanted to find something that was just hers – a task that would fill her time and use her creativity. She wistfully thought of the years she had spent as a young woman painting the flowers in the meadow and longed to pick up her paintbrushes once more. But how, when her paints were dried and her paintbrushes stiff with age?

Before we delve into the silviculture of how to cultivate success, I just want to pause for a second and think about some of the language we often use with reference to our career, our working lives and our passions. If you do a search online of 'how to find success in your career', you'll likely return lots of articles about how to achieve 'mastery'. In fact, in my original plan for this chapter was all about achieving just that. But here's the thing – the idea of 'mastery' includes some problematic language, implying an approach that's deeply embedded in the patriarchy. Completely at odds with our nourishing and immersive approach to nature, it speaks of control, and domination, and superiority, and that's not a corner of the woods I would choose to linger in.

This means there are two levels to career and working with our passions, in my experience. The first level is where you can immerse yourself in something that you love, just for the sheer joy of it, without thinking about earning a living. I can't help thinking of my friend Michelle. In all the years I have been writing, Michelle has been learning to play the guitar – not because she dreams of becoming a famous guitarist who earns a lot of money, but because she loves it. Her daily work may not be her passion, but those hours and minutes after she leaves the workplace are. If that is what inspires you, and you have no wish to 'achieve mastery' and conquer the world, then I would encourage you to skip over this section and meet us at the next crossroads. However, if being an expert or a master of something is where you want to be, and you want to do it without layers of self-loathing, then read on.

As human beings, we tend to compare ourselves with other people and, inevitably, it's a mistake. If you look at other people's careers and achievements, invariably you end up with half a story, which can make you feel short changed and hard done by when you consider your own efforts. Yet the truth is, there is no such thing as sudden triumph. In nature, nothing flowers without having undergone a significant period of growth and transformation first – it may have happened underground and out of sight, but that doesn't mean it wasn't being worked away at over a long period of time. For every successful debut novelist, you will find a drawer of unpublished manuscripts. For every best actor award, you will probably discover a lifetime's worth of night-school classes or a beginning that gave someone the privilege they needed to succeed. And for every story of a businessperson who has defied the odds and become a millionaire – Bill Gates, Steve Jobs, Karren Brady and Richard

Branson – there is another that came from a wealthy family which not only gave them what they needed to get started, introducing them to the right people at the right time, but also bailed them out when things went wrong.

While that might be wonderful for the very few, for most of us the path to success is paved with good old-fashioned graft and tenacity and can be hindered by these unrealistic tales of overnight success, as they make us feel inadequate. You don't have to take my word for it. When the comedian Bill Bailey was lauded in the press as 'an overnight success', his response was brilliantly telling: 'Twenty-two years I've been doing this comedy lark, so it's been like a meteoric rise to fame . . . if the meteor was being dragged by an arthritic donkey across a ploughed field, in northern Poland.'

So, if hard graft and dogged determination are the only ways to achieve success, just how long can we expect to be working for it? Chris Cancialosi, an expert in leadership and organisational development, cites the work of Malcolm Gladwell, who wrote that expert knowledge of a topic or skill, such as painting or music or even a sport like swimming, takes 10,000 hours of intensive study. That sounds like quite a commitment, doesn't it? It means it is important to ensure that you are committing your time to the right cause to begin with. If you are intending to grow to the top of the tree in getting to know something, it needs to be a topic that really inspires you. Also, it's important not to be downhearted if that thing is not your career – not all of us get to earn money doing the thing we love most. And if your passion isn't able to support you, it doesn't mean it is unworthy of your time and effort.

But the road to that much depth of understanding requires more than just time – you also need to have spent time with the right teachers and been given the right kind of feedback to help you grow, even if finding those teachers also becomes a challenge. When I needed my first teacher of witchcraft, I sat down on a rock by the seashore and sent an appeal to the universe for one: sure enough, two weeks later I found my teacher on an online forum. However, I am aware that life isn't always an exercise in ideas of 'universal ordering' – most of us are limited by geographic location (at that point I lived in London, where I had access to most things), or by the money we have available to pay for a teacher. While Wiccan coven training does not incur a fee – once you are on the path to initiation, we have a very strict code of not charging for training – that doesn't mean I can work for free. In the world of Wicca, we make a distinction between coven training (one on one with a big commitment on the part of both the teacher and the prospective initiate) and 'public' training, where people pay to attend a class on a particular topic.

So, there is the time and the money, but what about that feedback that you need as part of the process of learning to be an virtuoso? After all, adepts aren't born, they have to earn the right. As Cancialosi writes:

> To truly make this work, you have to remain keenly aware of your opportunities for improvement after every practice session. Without intentionally improving each and every time, you may end up working tirelessly, only to refine a less than desirable set of patterns.

In order to achieve knowledge of our chosen passion or field, we have to rewire our thinking and the only way to do that is by repetitive practice that includes a 'pattern interrupt' every time the result is less than perfect. This can be a real challenge to the ego. Think about those musicians hailed as geniuses, and how many hours of practice they have put in every day with the guidance of their teachers, or those sports stars who spent every morning and evening being taught by a coach before and after school. They may have had a natural ability to get them started, but they also had to put in the hours, take the (sometimes painful) feedback and then modify their work as a result. That feedback can sometimes feel like failure, but even the most accomplished geniuses fail – and then they try again. I have always loved the work of Leonardo da Vinci (who doesn't?), but he didn't always get it right. In 2017 I was lucky enough to see some of his works up close at an exhibition in London. The precision of the measurements he made and recreated in everything he studied, from a horse's ass to a cadaver, and his ability to capture a split second of motion and freeze it in time, are extraordinary. The one area he didn't seem to succeed in, however, was his drawings of water flowing into a pond – the water droplets appear solid and whole, without flow, but he kept trying again and again.

This need for continual practice and reassessment might sound relentless, but it isn't at all intended to dissuade you from working towards expertise in your chosen field. But expertise – mastery – isn't necessarily the only way to approach your passion. You can lean into it, and give yourself permission to enjoy something without making it an ordeal. While having a passion in life that gets you out of bed every morning (or that draws you into the evening) can be a true gift, if you want to take this level of knowledge to the next level, you won't find it waiting for you under a tree – you will have to go out and find it, and work at it every day. As Elizabeth Gilbert, author of *Eat Pray Love*, recounts in her book *Big Magic: Creative Living Beyond Fear*, she set aside some time every day in her twenties to write – to practise scenarios and descriptions, and just so she could stay close to writing. Gilbert isn't alone in this: every book I have written has been completed by doing just a little bit each day. Even my PhD thesis was written on the tube going to work each morning, so little and often can yield a bountiful summer harvest.

Yet this isn't only a journey for people at the beginning of their careers and in their early twenties. Countless people have found success at their chosen craft later on in life. Julie Dunne – once a successful accountant – is now (aged fifty-seven) absorbed in field expeditions and scientific research for the world-wide environmental organisation Earthwatch. Toni Morrison, author of *Beloved*, had her first novel published at the age of forty, winning a Pulitzer Prize at fifty-four. Stuart Firestein, once a theatre practitioner, is now a neuroscientist at Columbia University in New York, having made the leap in his late thirties. Then there is my personal favourite, Maggie Brookes, a former journalist who wrote poetry all her life and taught creative writing, nurturing countless other writers (me included). Her novels *The Prisoner's Wife* and *Acts of Love and War* came out with a major publisher just after she retired from teaching. Age is never a barrier to success and doing the thing you love most. But how do we find that passion? One way is to follow the path of your inspiration.

TRY THIS: CREATING A LIBRARY OF INSPIRATIONAL EXPERIENCES

In Wicca, my spiritual life and my creative life are two sides of the same coin. In my coven, we take it in turns to write each ritual anew, keeping the flow of energy alive. However, creative energy is a bit like a herb garden – you need to keep tending the plants, weeding, watering and nourishing them to be able to harvest their herby loveliness at the other end. One of my favourite ways to fertilise and feed my own creativity is to create a Book of Inspiration, a folder in which I keep favourite poems, pictures, quotations and so on. However, this visual approach may not work for you if you are someone who favours other sensory systems.

So instead, I would invite you to play around with your inspiration sources and your sensory system, and try to find a new favourite each month or quarter. If music floats your boat, commit to creating a new playlist for yourself every few months, one that will carry you away into your creativity. I have a classical playlist, including tracks such as *The Lark Ascending* by Vaughan Williams and Beethoven's Piano Concerto No. 5, which is uplifting and relaxing. If it's not music, but food that awakens your senses, then commit to creating a brand-new dish you've never cooked before each month. Buy some ingredients you've never tried and do some research into how they are used. If you prefer moving your body and you love running or swimming, try out a new path or a new swim spot (safely and with friends!). To enjoy the night sky, take yourself out of the city to a spot where you can gaze at the heavens without the impingement of light pollution. If it's artworks, go and try out an exhibition of artists you are not familiar with. Our brains need to create new neural pathways or they quickly become bored.

When you have experienced these ideas, record them in some way so that you can come back to them later when you feel flat. Write them in your notebook, record yourself a voice note, take photographs – capture the moment in whatever way works for you. And then go out and try something new again.

Spending time in your Library of Inspirational Experiences can be truly nourishing. If I am down, it cheers me; if I feel depleted, it recharges my batteries; and if I am needing a little inspiration for a new piece of writing or new ritual, it is these experiences that spark my imagination. The trick is to make sure that, whenever it starts to feel a little old and stale, you add in or swap out some experiences, reorganising your selection and trying something different. If you do one new thing each month, you will soon have dozens of new experiences to look back on.

READING THE MAP: YOU DON'T HAVE TO DEFINE YOURSELF BY HOW YOU EARN A LIVING

Elizabeth couldn't help wondering why it was that things had seemed so much easier when she was younger. Her joy was so much easier to find, when she had so few cares in the world, but now she was getting older, and knew the true cost of living a life where she had to be responsible and think about where the next meal would come from. How could she get back in touch with her younger self without losing control of her world?

All through my twenties and my first career choice, I thought I was a colossal failure because I found it impossible to earn my living doing what I loved. Granted, at that point I was a professional actor – and I had my Equity card to prove it – but the earnings declaration I sent in each year was pitiful. In my final submission, I realised I had only earned a second-hand umbrella as an actor that entire year, handed to me at an audition when I got caught in the rain. The last straw came when I attended an audition for yet another unpaid acting job and realised I had met the casting lead before.

'Thanks for keeping my details on file,' I said to her.

'Oh, that's OK. I always keep a list of people who will work for nothing,' she replied, not missing a beat. 'I know how tough it is out there,' she continued. 'I work for a casting director, and I see all the headshots and CVs going straight in the bin every morning.'

If ever there was a moment when you expect tumbleweed to blow through your woodland glen, it was then. I went home and decided I had to make some serious changes. Not because I had fallen out of love with acting, but because I had fallen out of love with the business and the way it was treating me. So, if your chosen industry is not treating you well, you don't have to stay in it. You always have choices and can choose to leave and take your skills elsewhere.

Don't let my experiences suggest to you that you can't earn a living being creative or working freelance. That demon voice is one I have been battling for years. There are plenty of people who manage it, although it helps if you have at least one stable income in your household. Some of us choose to maintain a day job while we make things on the side – it can really take the pressure off your relationship with your passion if you are not relying entirely on that to pay the mortgage. And yes, that means that I do wake up at 5 a.m. to write before I start work at the charity, but I love writing so much that I am happy to perform this act of service to the gods of creativity. It also brings another bonus for me – I am up and about with the lark, so I can steal a march on everyone else and experience the wonders of nature before most people are awake, either through the window of my writing room or by getting out in it. For me, this daily practice does wonders for my sense of equilibrium and momentum.

And what if we refuse to equate our success, usefulness and sense of identity with what we are paid to do and how much we earn? These days, if someone asks me what I do, I smile and ask them, 'Do you mean what do I do, or what do I do to earn money?' The lie that we have been sold by a capitalist patriarchal society is that money equals self. And, as I came to realise, it's just not true. If you are sustaining a day job while maintaining the creative work that sustains you, you're in good company. From Sir Arthur Conan Doyle (who was a surgeon) and Margaret Atwood (a barista) to Charlotte Brontë (a governess) and Stephen King (a janitor), there are many examples of inspiring and brilliant people who for many years kept both paths open.

If flow is what you need, and you want to give yourself all the methods of reaching it that are possible, then I also want to share with you my recipe for path-opener oil. This is the closest thing I know to flow in a bottle . . . particularly when you are heading down a particular path in the woods, and need the energy to continue flowing in the right direction (instead of going against it so you end up paddling upstream).

TRY THIS: A RECIPE FOR PATH-OPENER OIL

Most magical traditions that work with herbs and oils have various recipes for oils, incenses and brews to help with whatever life throws our way. This recipe for a path-opener oil is a personal favourite that I use whenever my way through the woods feels blocked or I'm mired in a sense of 'stuckness'.

The Hindu god Ganesh is known for his ability to clear obstacles. So, in one particular instance, when it felt as though my research work was floundering at every turn, I determined to dedicate myself to working with him every day for a calendar month. Each day I would create something for him – an oil, a necklace, an incense – or I would chant to him.

This oil was one of the first items I created: every time I felt frustrated or thwarted I would put some of it on my pulse points, or add it to a bath, an oil burner or even my floor wash. The results of this spell were far more successful than I could possibly have imagined. You could say it was a placebo effect and all in my mind, or you could go to the other extreme and say it was Ganesh working his magic. Or perhaps a combination of the two gave me the confidence to keep pushing onwards in new directions I had not considered before. Either way, it worked for me, and Ganesh now sits in every room of my home, at the heart of everything.

You will need:

* Half a cup of base oil, such as olive oil or a vegetable-based oil

* Ten drops of orange essential oil
* Ten drops of pine essential oil
* Ten drops of vetivert essential oil
* A sprig of sage (or a teaspoon of dried sage)
* A sprig of lavender (or a teaspoon of dried lavender)
* A sprig of rosemary (or a teaspoon of dried rosemary)
* A pinch of salt
* Half a teaspoon of frankincense pearls

Mix all of the ingredients together and place them in a bottle. Glass is best, as it won't soak up the oil in the way that plastic can. Coloured glass is even better as it prevents the essential oils from losing their scent. If you don't have coloured glass, just make sure you store your mixture out of direct sunlight.

The oil is ready to use straight away. You can use it as I did, perhaps with your own deity, archetype or inspirational figure in mind, or use it to anoint candles, as in the ritual at the end of this chapter.

Then make sure you go out and take practical action towards fulfilling your goals: send in that job application, drop an email to that professor, set up a new outlet for sharing your creations. Get out there and do the thing you love.

EMBARKING ON THE JOURNEY: SECOND CAREERS AND PADDLING DOWNSTREAM

One day Sam and Puck disappeared together, and Elizabeth could not find them anywhere in the forest. The woods remained quiet that day, their voices lost. At nightfall, just as Elizabeth was stirring a hot soup over a fire, they appeared between the trees, looking weary but triumphant.

'Where were you both?' she asked, trying but failing to hide a note of irritation in her voice.

Sam remained silent, but reached into his bag and drew out a neatly wrapped gift, handing it to her. She could tell by its shape and weight that it must be a book, and her heart lifted at the thought of what might be in its pages.

If you were to place an imaginary pendulum between cause at one end (where you are the driver of your own life and all its myriad decisions) and effect at the other (where you are the absolute victim of everything that happens), where would you sit? Do you tend to lurch from one situation to another feeling as if life – especially when it comes to your career – is something that is being 'done to you'? Or are you aware of the micro-choices you have made that have led you to where you are today? Perhaps you sit somewhere in between?

On the one hand, so much of the shape of our lives is not determined by us and it can often feel as if we have no agency. The reality of living in a Western economy in the twenty-first century is that the cost of living is spiralling, and many aspects that were once a given – affordable housing, free university education and healthcare and a 'job for life' – are no longer available. We are simply not operating in the post-war society that put measures in place to try to create a flourishing life for all.

Of course, the flip side is that we are left with a set of expectations that we can really struggle to fulfil when the dice are weighted against us from the outset. For example, the spiralling value of property and rising cost of mortgages make it hard for many people to make it onto the property ladder, something they might have taken for granted twenty years ago. I am inviting you to give yourself a bit of a break here, and realise you are doing the best you can. On the plus side, many of us are no longer lusting after a job for life (even though a sense of stability remains appealing). And – to go back to that pendulum – there remain so many things that we can do to shape where our careers take us next. We do not have to feel constantly buffeted by a storm outside of our influence.

If you can't help feeling that you should have tried any number of different career paths by this point (before remembering not to 'should' all over yourself), then perhaps it is time to stop thinking, 'I wonder what my life would have been if I had taken that course/ tried that idea/set up that business/contacted that person.' As one of my swimming buddies always tells me, 'You always regret the swim you didn't do, not the swim you did.'

Before you start shifting in your seat, don't worry. This is not one of those books that will urge you to throw everything aside and 'trust the universe to provide' while you jump over a precipice, your bills unpaid as you slowly lose everything. That approach might work if you have a safety net, but throwing off an income on a whim isn't great adulting in our current economic climate. Things can be more measured than that. Instead, I would urge you to find ways of bringing your passion into your day-to-day life. Spend one hour a week absorbed in it, if that's all you can manage to begin with, and I promise you won't regret it. Begin your day with thirty minutes of your favourite activity before work, and the working day will start to feel less onerous. Your sense of peace and equilibrium will increase tenfold; as your sense of spiritual and creative wellbeing increases, so will your physical and mental health. And, of course, if the only thing standing between you and your life's passion is the feeling that you have left it too late or that you are too old for that kind of thing, let's set that idea to one side.

But what happens if you have been trying to make that move into another life path and finding that you get blocked at every turn? If that path-opener oil we made doesn't seem to have opened the right doors, and all your firm intentions just aren't progressing things? There was a time when, having completed an MA and being well under way in my PhD, I was *sure* I wanted to make a move into academia. However, it became clear in my interviews that teaching experience in a university setting was going to be essential to securing a role, whereas my teaching experience was all community based and my PhD place didn't include enough regular teaching to qualify. The only way to gain the experience I needed would have been to give up a secure permanent job to try for a zero-hours teaching gig, surrendering the only regular source of income I had for a very unstable and capricious one. What was it that my gods wanted me to do? I was so sure that working in a university was the way forward. When I meditated on the tarot cards, picking out a selection with this very thing on my mind, I got the Swan, the Spider, Love, the Butterfly and Birth/Rebirth. All cards connected to creativity and transformation, suggesting that I was on the right path. I needed to reframe.

While I was looking outside myself for an opportunity to teach, I was forgetting that I already was teaching, albeit in a different environment – at a witchcraft bookshop. I was desperately seeking the answers outside myself, and yet the answers are usually found inside our own selves and circumstances. As one of my favourite pieces of pagan poetry says, 'If that which you seek you find not within yourself, you will never find it without.' Yet, undeterred, I kept trying to switch career, and it took me a few more months to catch on. Rather than forcing my way into a different kind of teaching role, I could keep developing my work in the bookshop instead. This took time to evolve – at first, my classes had five people, then over time it grew to ten, then to twenty . . . and before I knew it, the room was two circles deep in people wanting to join in. While I had been looking outside my experience to develop something new, what I was seeking was right there under my nose the whole time.

It might sound counterintuitive, but I was learning to stop trying. 'Trying' presupposes failure. If you are using the words 'I will try', you are already allowing for the possibility that you will fail;

if you allow that possibility to exist, your unconscious mind will hook onto it and before you know it that is what you'll have created. Sometimes the only way to navigate your way forwards is to take the path of least resistance, as the effort of going any other way is excruciating, taking up vast amounts of energy. As the inspirational speaker Esther Hicks has said, 'Nothing that you want is upstream . . . And you don't even have to turn the boat and paddle downstream, just let go of the oars, the current will carry you.'

It is downstream, or down the path of least resistance, that you might discover something magical you had not considered before. One summer morning when I was alone in my local temperate rainforest, I suddenly noticed a gate that I'd seen many times before but never stepped through. 'I wonder where that gateway leads?' I thought and, ever the disciple of Oscar Wilde, I can resist everything except temptation. Pushing the gate easily open, taking a deep breath and putting my best foot forward, I set off in search of adventure, Bilbo Baggins style. What I found may not have been a dragon's hoard or a doorway into Rivendell, but it was a wonder all of its own. A woodland path led down to a river, surrounded on both sides by wood anemones, tall swaying foxgloves and birdsong, and winding my way along its banks I found what would become my sacred spot – that favourite icy pool that I have returned to again and again: the Witches' Spa.

If, like me, you feel as if you have been battering your head on the door so hard to be let in to your career path that it hurts, perhaps now is the time to surrender that energy and begin by allowing your inner guide to take you instead. Let your sense of wonder and curiosity take the reins with a spirit of openness to what the world might already be bringing you.

But what can you do if you feel so hopelessly lost in the woods that every path seems fraught and hard going? That's when witches tend to take out their divinatory tools . . .

KNOWING WHAT WE DON'T KNOW

'We thought you might like this,' Sam told the imperfect goddess, looking to Puck for a nod of affirmation. 'But we had to go all the way to the town to get it.'

Elizabeth ripped open the paper, a feeling of excitement coiled in her belly. She looked at the spine of the book she had unwrapped. The Book of Pigments by A. J. Cressida. Uncertain as to what this was, she riffled through the pages, and it started to dawn on her. The book told her everything she needed about creating her own paints, using the plants and stones and herbs of the forest.

Elizabeth had thought the only way to get new paints was to buy them, but now she realised that oak galls would create an ink, that sage leaves could be steeped to produce a green dye. Annatto seed would create an orange paint, while elderberries and blackberries could be crushed and mixed with water to create a deep burgundy colour. She had so much to learn and experiment with, but all she needed was right here.

In witchcraft classes, we often quote the epigraph carved above the gateway to the Temple of Apollo at Delphi in ancient Greece – 'Know Thyself'. This temple housed the Delphic oracle, the priestess who would dispense predictions and wisdom to the wealthy and determined people who would make their way to her. Of course, the Temple of Apollo is now in ruins, and the Delphic oracle no longer exists, so what do you do if you want to find out what you don't know?

Witches in training tend to choose a favourite form of divination. This is where you will have to forgive me, because if you haven't encountered some of these ideas before, there's no way of describing them without sounding like a class at Hogwarts. The forms of divination were as varied as my own Wiccan teachers – everything from psychometry (where you hold an object and tell the story of it that comes into your conscious awareness) to scrying using ink poured into water.

As you'll have gathered, my favoured method is tarot. When you begin learning tarot it can seem overwhelming, with seventy-eight cards, each with its own layered meanings and any number of interpretations depending on where it is placed in a reading.

My first tarot teacher, Phoenix, had a very vivid way of teaching the meanings of the cards. He encouraged us to take one of the Major Arcana (of which there are twenty-two) each week and spend as much time in that card's company as we could. We were to carry it with us everywhere we went and report back at the end of the week, sharing with the class how the card had shown up in our daily lives. It was quite uncanny how their themes would manifest in the real world. Consequently, there were three cards – Death, the Tower and the Devil – that we were all dreading. These are known as the bad boys of tarot. If one shows up in your reading, then you know you are in for a change of some kind – and usually one you haven't chosen. Phoenix's solution for this trepidation was to have us carry all three at once. His rationale was this: if you are going to have a difficult time, you might as well get it all done as quickly as possible. Yet you'll know from looking at those cards in previous chapters that they are not as deadly or as dark as you may have heard.

What divination can offer is a sense of what is happening around you, of which you might not be consciously aware. I don't believe the knowledge comes from an outside or supernatural source; I don't believe the cards themselves necessarily have agency. They are a tool. In other words, tarot can help bring to light what is lurking in the shadows of your consciousness and you have the free will to decide which future you want to create with that understanding.

When it comes to choosing those cards, the ways in which we place them and the order in which we choose them is important. If we put them down randomly, the meanings can become confused and woolly. We need a framework, a layout, where each position represents a context or connected idea. In the last tarot course I attended, with the fabulous Suzanne Corbie, one of the homework exercises was to design our own reading layout. I designed a reading that was intended to help me navigate life when I feel a little lost. I called it 'The Way through the Woods'. Each card laid down is intended to illustrate something hidden regarding the problem I am facing and helps me mark a logical and linear route through any given situation. There's a diagram of the layout opposite so that you can see what I mean.

TRY THIS: A WAY THROUGH THE WOODS READING TO HELP YOU NAVIGATE YOUR PATH

You will need:

* An oracle or tarot deck of your choice
* Your notebook and pen to record what you discover

Find yourself a quiet spot where you won't be disturbed and take a few deep breaths to steady yourself. Spend a few moments thinking about the question you want to ask the cards and see if you can formulate it into a single enquiry. The answer you get will be as clear as your question, so if your thoughts are racing and leaping around like little forest goats, the answer will be too. It's OK for it to be open-ended, however. Sometimes, rather than asking a specific question, I just think, 'Thank you for telling me what I need to know about X', while shuffling the deck. Once you have thought and shuffled as much as you feel you need to, lay out the cards like this:

7. Possible outcome

6. Advice

5. Challenges sent to test you

3. Blockages and weaknesses

2. Where you want to be

4. Strengths

1. Where you are now

By all means look up interpretations of what the cards mean, but try not to be too glued to these explanations. Instead, allow your childhood self to tell you a story based on what the pictures are showing you. What meanings does that story suggest to you? Or what images and associations come to mind as you look at that card? As you sit with the reading and the position of the cards, you will begin to get a sense of what it is you need to know and to take away from the session.

I recently did a reading for a friend who was stuck in a seemingly impossible situation, waiting for an exit route from a professional bind. Despite several of us urging that they already had a way out (by calling a halt to the situation and leaving by the nearest exit), the person felt honour bound to try everything they possibly could to resolve it, even though the stress was making them ill.

When I did a reading on this, to help figure out what it was that we weren't seeing, I pulled the Prince of Cups (an open-hearted traveller who is trying to remain honourable) at the first position. Position two showed the Death card which, in spite of its fearsome reputation, simply indicates an ending, and desperately wanting the situation to come to a close. At the third position was the Emperor, indicating a need to follow the rules. My friend was following their ethical code to the letter, and it was blocking their progress. The strength position (number four) showed the Prince of Wands – the ability to take an idea and really run with it, however, in this instance, my friend was waiting for an act of aggression on the part of the opposition which would allow them to move on – and was therefore stymied. The challenge presented in position six was the Eight of Swords, which indicates a self-imposed prison. The illustration depicts a woman blindfolded and bound, standing surrounded by eight swords. What she doesn't see is an immediate way out, just by her left foot. All she really needs to do is take a side step and she will be free. The advice card was the Three of Pentacles – the indication being that the person needed to return to their creative activities, as they are a skilled craftsperson producing beautiful work. The outcome was the Magician – my friend had all the tools and skills they needed at their disposal. Again, all they had to do was give a little leap and allow the magic to happen. As is so often the way, sometimes we need to give ourselves permission to believe and get out of the way while it happens.

Now, if tarot isn't your thing, take yourself off to those woods in person to work out (or walk out!) a particularly knotty sense of career blockage. As someone who has always struggled with seated meditation, I find this moving version much easier to work with. As your walk progresses, you'll find that you move from a state of constant 'inner chatter' to one of more peaceful contemplation. Our thinking, logical brain is the one we use to problem-solve, but it's our creative unconscious that has so many of the solutions – and that's what we're trying to connect with here. The unconscious speaks the language of feelings and symbols, those non-verbal cues that tap us on the shoulder but then disappear into the undergrowth if we try to look at them directly. The rhythm of the movement will help you to get quiet enough to hear this inner compass – the quiet voice that whispers to you. In the rush and flurry of modern life, we often talk over that voice, or dismiss it as a silly idea, or else don't listen at all. Allow that inner voice to speak, ask it to share its secrets with you. You won't regret it, I promise.

NAVIGATING IMPOSTER SYNDROME – IS IT REAL OR IMAGINED?

Over the next few months, the imperfect goddess spent every spare moment between the covers of her book. She was determined to create paints for herself, but when she went out into the woods to search for the ingredients, it was not as she had imagined. The sage had been munched by slugs, the elders were not yet in fruit, holding tight to their flower heads. At last she managed to gather some woody oak galls, left vacant by the wasps that had emerged the year before. Determined to carry on, she gathered a handful of the hard, round cases and took them back home to crush. She would have to be careful, as there were not many remaining.

The imperfect goddess began to feel like a failure, and when Sam and Puck looked at her enquiringly on her return, she felt even worse. She had once been such a good artist, but time and tide had moved on and it felt as if her ability had grown dusty with neglect. Perhaps she would have to work harder than she had thought. It had all seemed so easy when she was a child, unconcerned with getting everything just right.

'Yes, I am studying for an MA, but I am not very academic,' I found myself saying to a friend one day. She looked at me archly over the top of her coffee cup.

'At what point do you think you might be academic enough?' she asked. She had hit the nail on the head. In fact, even late into my PhD studies, I found myself repeating the same mantra: 'I am doing a PhD, but I am not very academic.' My partner, who is a historian, often hears me saying the same thing. Recently, we were discussing a line-up of people we might consider interviewing for a project. Each time we came to a name in the list I considered more 'highbrow', I added them to his pile. Is it because he has worked in a university, while I haven't? Is it because his topic is history, while mine is more creative? Or is it (insert drum roll here) because he is male?

If I look at the evidence, my whole life has been subject to variations on this theme, setting myself the strangest measures of success. At one time I was convinced I could only be considered a 'proper writer' when I started to earn money from writing professionally. That might seem like a reasonable goalpost, yet I spent ten years writing before I earned a single penny from it. So what was I doing every day, getting up at an ungodly hour to ensure I had time to write? Did that not constitute 'proper' writing?

If you have felt that you don't deserve to be where you are, that you haven't earned the success you've experienced, that one day someone will realise that it's all been a terrible mistake, then you are not alone. The idea of Imposter Syndrome, or Imposter Phenomenon as it was originally labelled, was identified in a study in 1978 by psychologists Pauline Rose Clance and Suzanne Imes. Clance and Imes originally conceived that only women suffer from Imposter Phenomenon, but our understanding of the subtleties of this problem have since become more nuanced. For example, today we are better able to understand that it's not a fault in the person who experiences these feelings – it's a fault in the system. As Ruchika Tulshyan and Jodi-Ann Burey write in their article for *Harvard Business Review*, 'Stop Telling Women They Have Imposter Syndrome':

> The impact of systemic racism, classism, xenophobia, and other biases was categorically absent when the concept of imposter syndrome was developed. Many groups were excluded from the study, namely women of color and people of various income levels, genders, and professional backgrounds. Even as we know it today, imposter syndrome puts the blame on individuals, without accounting for the historical and cultural contexts that are foundational to how it manifests in both women of color and white women.

151

> Imposter syndrome directs our view toward fixing women
> at work instead of fixing the places where women work.

Some 70 per cent of us will suffer from imposterism at some point in our lives, and if you are a person of colour or a member of a minority culture or a male who experienced a lot of criticism at a formative age, it's even more likely that you'll encounter it. Yet labelling these feelings as 'imposter syndrome' can even make them even harder to bear. The language carries with it a whiff of fraudulence, and that can lead to a vicious cycle.

The answer then is in the wider context, so a longer-term solution requires that we look at those workplace settings and affect widespread change when it comes to who feels welcome and valued. We need to foster truly diverse workplaces that allow all genders and ethnicities to flourish and to recognise the validity of these feelings.

Nevertheless, if we are battling with our sense of self-worth right now and we can't, as an individual, change society overnight, what can we do to work with these thoughts? Dr Samantha Boardman, who writes for *Psychology Today*, says that she felt like a fraud when she was sent on hospital rounds as a newly qualified doctor. She came up with one lovely solution, keeping a handwritten thank-you notecard from a patient in the pocket of her doctor's coat. Whenever imposter syndrome reared its ugly head, she would reach for it. 'Over time,' she says, 'it frayed and crumpled and a coffee spill made some of the words illegible. But it didn't matter. I had memorised them by then and just knowing it was there made all the difference.'

As well as hanging onto the words of those who truly appreciate your skill and creativity in the workplace, there is nothing wrong with admitting when you are not sure about something. It can be seen as a great strength to be willing to enquire further before you give a definitive answer.

In my own craft, I have also had to take this sense of where I should limit myself in hand. I always said that I would never want to run my own coven or be a high priestess – I was happy living in the shadows and keeping myself small. However, the gods have a way of pushing us on towards things that mean we sometimes have to step outside our comfort zone, even when that's not where we think we are going. (Hint: I now co-run my own coven of witches and I am happy to report that I intend to carry on doing so.)

TRY THIS: A COMMITMENT TO YOUR LIFE'S FLOW

The written word can carry a magical significance – long before all of us learned to read and write, people would carry scraps of paper inscribed with the written word as a form of magical amulet. For some it was quotations from the Bible, for others unknown words that they believed held power. Speaking those words aloud has a further resonance that echoes our unconscious need for ritual and enchantment. Whether you say them as a vow to your divine helpers, to the natural world or just to hear yourself say them out loud, it can mean the difference between knowing something is a possibility and stating it as a certainty.

You can do this ritual alone if you prefer, but I would encourage you to get together with a friend (or three), as you can then bear witness to each other's commitment to living your life to its greatest fulfilment from hereon in. Before you start, think about the vow you intend to make to yourself, so that you can put it into words when the moment comes.

You will need:

* Your bottle of path-opener oil (see page 138)

* A red candle
* A gold candle
* Some paper
* A pen that you enjoy writing with
* A glass of something delicious for toasting

The red and gold colours of the candles are significant. Red is the colour of assertion and confidence, in pre-modern planetary magic it is associated with Mars, the bringer of courage. Gold signifies the planet Sol – the sun – the body associated with success and sovereignty. You are therefore encouraging your unconscious self to step into the light of its courage.

Red and gold are also associated with my companion deity, Ganesh. As with all of our rituals, these are intended as sacred moments in your everyday life. I would therefore encourage you to clean the space you'll be working in and cleanse yourself too. A salt bath is always my favourite way of preparing for a personal ritual. Then dress comfortably in something soft that makes you feel good. We are looking for maximum comfort and nurturing, not a feeling of discomfort or constriction.

When you are ready, light extra candles or tea lights around the room and switch out or dim the electric lights. Take the two coloured candles, anoint them with six drops of the path-opener oil and carefully light them.

Next, take your piece of paper and write the following statement on it with today's date:

> I, [insert your name here], commit to myself [and my gods, if you'd like to name them] that from here onwards, I commit my time and my energy to [state your commitment here]. This I take as

my solemn vow to myself. I will allow nothing to
hinder or prevent me from fulfilling this oath.

When you have finished writing and are happy, transform
your words into a spoken oath and say your life's purpose
statement out loud. If you are completing the ritual with
a friend, allow each other the space to do this and really
encourage one another in the endeavour. No half-measures
– we want full on enthusiasm from each of you.

When you each speak your oath, make sure you raise a
glass and toast to your success. Now, go get 'em, tiger!

CHAPTER SIX

THE JOURNEY IN SEARCH OF HOME AND BELONGING

Muses no more what ere ye be
In fancys pleasures roam
But sing (by truth inspir'd) wi' me
The pleasures of a home
Nor vain extreems I sigh for here
No Lordlings costly dome
'Be thine the choice' says reason 'where
'Contentment crowns a home'

John Clare

TAROT CARD: The Ten of Cups, the Six of Swords, the Four of Wands

Light filters through stained glass, dyeing the altar cloth shades of muted violet and red. A simple cross sits at the centre of the cloth, with very little adornment around it. Only a pair of candles stand guard each side. The door at the back of the church is open to a bright, sunny, Beltane morning, and the air is heavy with the sound of cars repeatedly driving over a drain cover. Ger-dunk. Ger-dunk.

Inside is peaceful. Red bench cushions echo the red carpet leading down the centre aisle, through a twelfth-century Norman sandstone chancel archway. I am completely alone.

It might surprise you that I would start this chapter on home inside a church. I am, after all, just visiting. Yet I've never been one to shy away from sacred space, whether that's a church, a mosque, a synagogue or a temple. I also know that I will find that same sense of grace sitting underneath a cherry tree or a sycamore or watching the river Wye gliding beneath the Monnow bridge in South Wales.

Yet how do we find that sense of peace, of the divine, in the places we call home each and every day? How can we identify *where* we will find that sense of belonging in this whole wide world? And why is it important?

LOCATING THE SENSE OF HOME

As time passed, Elizabeth became accustomed to waking each morning with a warm feeling of belonging. The forest was now as familiar to her as the place she had spent her childhood – she knew every glade and every path that wound around the trees to the water. If she stopped a while and listened very carefully, she could hear the voice of the forest whispering to her. It wasn't a frightening feeling – just a faint echo of a thought inside her mind that she knew wasn't hers. It welcomed her into the forest, as a human guardian for the creatures that lived there.

'Mother of the forest,' it breathed. 'Stay and be one with us.'

In modern pagan faiths, we refer to the spirit of a place, or its soul, as a distinct entity in itself. The spirit of a place can refer to several things. It can mean those aspects celebrated by artists and writers – written about in folk tales, celebrated in festivals, depicted in paintings. It can be connected to an appreciation of the tangible monuments, rivers, places of interest or traditional crafts to be found there. It can also refer to more spiritual elements (though I'd argue just as grounded) such as the ancient Roman idea of the *genius loci* – the protective spirit of a place – or the *lares*, the deified spirits of departed ancestors who watch over a household, and the *spiritus mundi*, the world spirit.

However you define them in your model of the world – gods, ancestors, spirits of nature, elementals, spirits of place or others – they are present around us, both in the natural world and in our homes. If you're open-minded, it is possible to foster a healthy, harmonious relationship with them. By doing this you can feel reassured you have an extra layer of defence in your home – someone else is keeping an eye on your wellbeing.

Some of my students have expressed nervousness about reaching out in this way to the spirit of a place using the exercise you'll find below. Rest assured, I'm not suggesting a ritual where, séance-like, you start hearing the voices of the land or conjure some kind of daemonic being. In pagan faiths, our gods are not presented as a binary version of good and evil. They, like us, are imperfect, but also creative, joyous, and full of humour. This means I'm less worried about being controlled by some kind of evil force, because the concept doesn't appear in my world.

The other thing to note is that when working with the gods or divine beings, you may not see or hear things with your physical senses (although some people do). Instead, in my experience, information often arrives as a 'download', with a piercing tone in one or both ears, followed by the growing sense that this piece of information has come from something outside of myself. Other times it's smaller ideas or images that drop in that weren't there before, or the feeling of receiving an answer to a question that I've been wanting to ask.

For example, the first time I flew over San Francisco I knew my trip there was going to be significant – I had wanted to visit since I first read Armistead Maupin as a teen and listened to Counting Crows and Mark Eitzel in my twenties. I felt as if I *knew* this place, even though I'd only ever seen it in films or on television. As the plane circled over the city that night, I had a really strong feeling that dropped into my awareness. It told me, 'You're very welcome here and you can visit as often as you like, but you will never make your home here' (and I haven't).

TRY THIS: CONTACTING THE SPIRITS OF PLACE

It helps if you're in the place whose spirit you'd like to connect with. Begin by finding a quiet spot where you will not be disturbed, preferably out in nature or a garden. If you are seated, place your feet on the ground; if you are lying down, ensure your spine is in contact with the earth, though it's fine to have a picnic blanket or a coat beneath you.

Start by taking three deep breaths, allowing your thoughts to settle. Don't worry if your mind begins presenting you with shopping lists or 'to-do' agendas, as so often happens when we are quiet. Just thank your unconscious self for these gifts and allow the thoughts to pass on through like clouds drifting across the sky.

If it's safe to close your eyes, do so now and allow your awareness to connect to your breath. You might notice how your body is feeling, but don't place a value judgement on this – it is neither good nor bad, it just is. Be aware of these thoughts as you continue to breathe as deeply as you can, feeling a sense of peacefulness and relaxation spreading down from the top of your head across your face and your cheeks, releasing the muscles around your eyes and your jaw. Allow the sense of serenity to move through your neck, your spine, across your back, your chest, your arms and on down to your legs.

Now, reach out with your awareness and become mindful of the environment around you. What sounds can you hear? What can you see behind your eyelids? How does the air taste to you? What can you feel? What can you smell? Are you in a natural space or a man-made one? How does that affect the sensory information you are receiving? Are you hearing nature, or the background hum of human life?

Next, reach out with your awareness for the non-sensory information. How does this place feel to you (emotionally and energetically rather than sensorially)? If it were to take the form of a being, what would it look, sound or feel like? If you were to have a conversation with it, what would you want to ask? What would you want it to reveal?

What would you like the spirit of the place to help you with? You can ask for its help, but don't be surprised if it asks for something in return. That might be to create an altar space in your home to honour it, or to remember it regularly. It might be to collect a bag of litter on your way home, or to join a local community group that works to protect the place. How will you choose to honour it in future?

PREPARING FOR THE JOURNEY: EXPLORING HOME AND A SENSE OF BELONGING

There came a time when the imperfect goddess and her man of the green-wood became aware that the animals in the forest around them were on the move.

'Where are they going?' Elizabeth asked Sam, when they saw another herd of ponies moving away into the distance. The forest all around them was starting to feel eerily quiet, the birds and their light summer chatter thinning away.

'Perhaps we should consult the spirit of the oak tree,' Sam suggested, 'for it is old and wise, and has many connections through the woods.'

Sam stayed with Puck, while Elizabeth journeyed to the heartwood of the forest, where she found its oldest oak. She stood in front of it, her hands touching its gnarled, knotted trunk.

'O wise spirit of the oak, I stand before you with a request for help,' said Elizabeth. 'Please can you tell me why the animals are leaving the forest? Where do they go?'

Elizabeth awaited the answer as her heart hammered, but the oak tree offered only silence. She was beginning to despair, but then a voice above her spoke.

There are only two places on this earth that (so far) I've been able to call home: Dartmoor and London. I lived in the city for twenty-eight years, and felt in service to the place as London's witch (or one of them). Yet every day of those years, I missed Dartmoor with an almost physical ache. I yearned for it with the sense of nostalgia and longing and loss encapsulated in the Welsh word *hiraeth*. As time went on, Dartmoor pulled ever more strongly on my heart.

Of course, I am not the first writer to experience that deep feeling of *hiraeth* for home – some of our best landscape writers have been motivated by the sense of exile, whether voluntary or enforced. But just why do we become attached to these specific places? Douglas Pocock – a former senior lecturer in geography at the University of Durham – explores the significance of landscape and how the concept of 'home' is formed during our childhoods. He posits that this attachment is developed by both the restriction and the repetition experienced during those first years, through which 'a crucial and indelible bond is established with early place or "home"'. Even though we may change our base many times in our lives, he argues that this very first early place 'remains the centre of our cosmos, containing our own unique, unrepeatable beginning. We may move, but we cannot begin a second time.'

This early perception of home becomes fused with identity and our ideas of belonging, and although young adults need to explore the wider world, once a person has left home they will often yearn for it, just as Thomas Hardy did for his native Wessex, James Joyce for Dublin, Mary Webb for Shropshire and D. H. Lawrence for Nottinghamshire. If you had met me in my twenties in a book-shop in London, likely I would have bored you rigid with tales of Dartmoor – and I am sure that there will be many of you who feel the same about your first home.

But what if you haven't had the privilege of a fixed home in childhood? Perhaps you have grown up in care, with foster families or as part of a family unit that moved around a lot. Despite what Pocock says, I know that for some people a deep feeling of connection comes instead from a specific *type* of place, rather than one particular location linked to your childhood. Perhaps for you that's a river in high summer, the throbbing streets of a bright city or an allotment in June full of more-than-human life.

The psychologist Marianna Pogosyan has noted that the need for a sense of belonging, while fundamental to our wellbeing, is also full of paradoxes – and isn't always about tying us to a single place. The safety of belonging can also help send us out into the world:

> We search for it everywhere – in the arms of kin, on familiar streets, among friends with similar beliefs. Yet, there it is – in solitude, in literature, among magnificent trees. Belonging anchors our hearts to our nests. Yet, there it goes – unfastening our wings and setting us free on our quests.

A study published in the *Australian Journal of Psychology* in 2020 showed that there are four significant components at play when it comes to this feeling of connection: competencies, opportunities, motivations and perceptions – all of which can be strengthened, and nurtured, no matter what our early childhood experiences were. Competencies relate to the skills we use to form relationships with others; opportunities to what we have available to us – are we seeking out chances to engage with others with similar interests? Motivation does what it says on the tin – we all need to belong, but how far are we willing to go in seeking that sense of home? Perception, possibly the most crucial quality of all, relates to how you see the world. Are you a glass-three-quarters-full person or do you tend to see the world through the prism of what is missing rather than what is present? If you are someone constantly battling with your inner Eeyore, here's an exercise for you . . .

TRY THIS: THE DESIRE PATH JOURNALING EXERCISE

While you may think that emotions are something that you feel and have no control over, the good news is that this simply isn't true. Emotions are very often directed by your thoughts. If your thinking is going down a negative spiral, then so will your feelings. And if this kind of thinking becomes habitual, it may feel as if anything different is impossible.

Belonging is something that happens over time – almost imperceptibly – but it's not unusual to feel a little disconnected from your sense of place and nature, and this can lead to feelings of isolation, loss of equilibrium and powerlessness. But when you walk through green areas such as city parks, have you noticed those 'new' paths worn through the grass that diverge from the designated route? These are called desire paths, formed over time by humans and animals when they see a short cut that seems more attractive or logical to them. This exercise is designed to 'plug you back in' to your surroundings and create a new desire path in your thinking.

The first step in changing your thoughts (and therefore your feelings) is to identify what the unhelpful thoughts have been, so that you can begin to put some reins on them. In the chain of our psychological make-up, thoughts drive feelings, which in turn drive behaviours. So, let's work backwards from there. Spend a little time with your journal and think about a recent time that you felt all at sea and bereft of connection, and maybe behaved in a way that identified how rootless you were feeling. For example, did you respond poorly to a situation at work because you were feeling alone and vulnerable? Perhaps you were defensive when someone made a suggestion about a change in your working practice, or you had a very long moan about the state of your home without coming up with any helpful suggestions for improvement, which is unlike you. Ask yourself these questions:

- What was the behaviour that you noticed?
- How did you feel immediately before you behaved in that way?
- What was the thought that occurred just before the feeling kicked in?

Don't spend too long thinking about this – the answer will usually be the first thing that pops into your mind. And if the trigger seems silly and pointless when you identify it, don't be surprised. Our brains do some odd things.

When we have experienced a trauma, it's not unusual for our thoughts to be affected by our stress responses to that experience, and we may start to catastrophise – it's how the primitive bits of our brains try to keep us safe. However, it's not always serving us for good if that negative energy is being misdirected, making us unable to see the good in ourselves and the world. For example, if you have left a place because of something bad that happened to you there, you may find that you expect that same trauma to occur in the new place too. You may not feel able to put down roots and get to know people because your thoughts are telling you that you won't be accepted there.

With that in mind, next, we are going to employ a technique designed by the ancient Greek philosopher Socrates in about 400 BCE. Yes, that's right, humans have been tackling the issue of the irrational monkey-brain for a long time. So ask yourself the following:

- Is this thought realistic?
- Am I basing my thoughts on facts or on feelings?
- What is the evidence for this thought?
- Could I be misinterpreting the evidence?
- Am I viewing the situation as unequivocal, when it's really more complicated?
- Am I having this thought out of habit, or do the facts support it?

Finally, do a little reframing. Taking that thought you have interrogated, ask yourself:

- What is the truth of the situation?
- What is really happening?
- If you were going to replace that destructive thought with a more helpful one – that new desire path – what would it be?

Keep a written record of these kinds of destructive thoughts as they arise, so that over time you'll have a reserve of new ways forward to help shift your perspective.

NAVIGATING CHANGE WITH THE HELP OF YOUR BODY

Just then Elizabeth heard a voice inside her mind, speaking to her just as clearly as the voice of the forest had. She looked up into the branches of the tree. There sat the owl, looking down at her with its wide-eyed stare. Was it the owl who spoke, or the voice of the forest?

'You are waiting for the answer from the oak tree, but the spirit of the oak has departed this place,' said the owl. Elizabeth heard the thought as clearly as if it were one of her own, but she knew it wasn't her voice that was speaking these words. She was perturbed.

'But why?' she asked, attempting to stifle a growing panic. 'Where has it gone?'

'The spirit of the oak has gone with the animals,' said the owl. 'People are coming, and so the forest will be felled to make way for farmland and houses. There is no longer a place for us here,' said the owl. 'You must go home now and ready yourself to leave,' the owl continued. 'I promised I would wait and tell you. Now my task is discharged.' And with this final word, the owl flew away like a ghost flitting among the trees.

When we're faced with having to make decisions about where to go to create or recreate that sense of belonging, the number of choices can feel overwhelming. What if I get this wrong? What if I choose to move, and it is the wrong choice? What if I choose the wrong place to move to? What would it feel like if you knew you had your very own guidance system, deep within your body, and that all you had to do was to learn to speak the language of your body so that you could pick up its cues, and follow the trail it led you on?

My NLP teacher David Shephard explained that humans tend to have a sensory system they favour – sight, sound, taste, smell or touch – as a way of understanding the world. For example, you might find it easiest to visualise things and find yourself using expressions such as 'I can really see what you mean'. Or perhaps you prefer audible input – the radio, audio books, spoken instruction – in which case you have a leading sense of sound. My leading sensory system is kinaesthetic. I detect my way through the world, relying on how something feels in my body when deciding where to go or what to do next. If I am ever unsure, I get quiet, go inside and check with my inner 'k'.

Whatever your own leading system, we can all use this same sense of inner 'k' to see (or hear) if something is the right choice for us. My friend Lizzie refers to this as 'checking your whiskers', since cats use theirs as a sensory measure of the world. What makes it difficult for us to check that inner sense of how something feels is that most of our lives are very busy – we tend to zoom from one experience to the next, just like my spaniel zooms around the house like a mad thing when she's just had a bath. We expend a lot of energy moving from one life challenge to the next, and sometimes forget that we need to stop, turn our attention inside and listen to the signals our bodies are giving us. A good walk in nature can help with this, or meditation, or time spent at your household altar, if you have one. Just pause, light a candle and allow your thoughts to drift on through like clouds, until you can start to feel the sensations around your body.

When I was considering my dramatic move to the south-west, my kinaesthetic whiskers were well and truly quivering, as you can see from my diary at the time:

30 March
An idea has taken root that I can't shake off. My job is becoming more and more remote, and I think it is time for

me to move back to Devon. If I am smart about it I wouldn't have to sever my ties to London. I could live and work from home down there and come up to London when I need. If I book my teaching dates around coven meetings, I could come up for a few concentrated days of work in London and then go home to Devon. Obviously, I need several miracles for this to happen, but the more I think of it, the more the 'k' feels absolutely right. I have vowed to my gods to surrender to the flow on this one. No more resistance. As if in answer to this, I heard skylarks in the land around Moat Mount Farm this morning, which is a first. I am used to hearing them on Dartmoor, but never in London.

In case you are wondering about the significance of the sound of skylarks (while being miraculous in London), it is that the move I had in mind was to a place called Skylark Rise. Coincidence or synchronicity? Portentous or merely noteworthy? I will let you decide.

The question of the mind–body connection is one that physicians and psychologists have been debating for decades: how are they linked? To what extent? And how much do they influence each other? In fact, up until the seventeenth century it was generally believed that the two were interconnected, with Western societies gradually pulling the mind and body apart into distinct entities over the subsequent 400 years. It's only in the twentieth century that psychologists and scientists started to connect the two again in earnest, looking to other parts of the globe for the physical and psychological tools that can get the mind and body working in harmony once more, whether tai chi, yoga, qigong or meditation.

They also began to look at how some illnesses and physical problems can have a psychological dimension. Our unconscious minds are in control of driving our bodies and filtering our sensory experiences for us – they literally breathe for you, move your muscles and do all the donkey work when you are learning, being creative, dreaming or making magic – but they can't communicate using language, because that's a function of the conscious mind. So is it any wonder that sometimes our bodies remind us, through physical symptoms, of what we need? During this time of deciding whether to relocate – and how – my sciatica flared up again, my hips began to hurt and lower-back pain thrummed. It didn't take too much pondering to sense a misalignment in my current situation and a deeply held fear of moving forwards.

One of the benefits of taking a problem to the woods, which of course is what this whole book is really about, is that you will start to become aware of little twangs and places of pain or discomfort as you walk. And if walking isn't accessible to you, then a hammock in a tree could be a delicious alternative. Ask your unconscious mind what it is trying to tell you, breathing into those aching places and spaces, and you might be surprised by how much insight you gain. If you are really stumped you could consult the Google oracle, and of course you must see a doctor if the discomfort is persistent, but – as with tarot or dream symbolism – I am a great fan of each of us asking what these images or messages from our bodies mean to *us*. Even if a relocation isn't on the cards for you right now, your body is always your first and only home. Be still enough for long enough to hear it speak.

BEGINNING THE JOURNEY: KNOWING WHERE TO GO

As Elizabeth watched the owl take flight, she felt uprooted suddenly, like a tree felled by a storm. Back under their beech tree, she related the words of the owl to Puck and Sam. There was worry in their eyes.

'Can I stay with you?' asked Puck, uncertain.

'Yes, of course!' said Elizabeth, smiling reassurance while feeling unsettled inside. 'But where should we go now?' she asked Sam.

Sam looked thoughtful for a moment and then he said, 'Perhaps we should have followed the animals. I wonder if it's too late?'

Just then a flock of sheep began to pick their way through the trees.

'Then let's follow the herd,' said Elizabeth, watching. 'Surely they will know where to go.'

So they packed up what little they had, and Elizabeth embraced the great trunk of the beech tree. She closed her eyes, trying to sense its spirit, but like all the others it had already gone from this place. All that was left was an empty wooden casing, and Elizabeth felt reassured. Maybe she would find her beech tree again wherever it was they were going.

When you live a life of dedication to the gods, they are very good at letting you know when something big and significant is coming. Of course, they don't tell you what it is specifically – that would be cheating and it would spoil the surprise – but you might well receive preparatory urgings like I did. Before I even realised that a relocation was on the cards, I started saving money and nesting, buying things for a home I didn't even have yet. Perhaps you are also beginning to come to the conclusion that you need to move on from where you're living right now, feeling in your bones (or your back!) that the time is fast approaching to get out of your bed early one morning, pack up your basket and head off to a new home. But how do you know which direction to head? Which path are you meant to be taking?

Most self-help books written from a more spiritual perspective would suggest at this point that you must transcend your physical fears and trust the universe to catch you, right? While I would love to be one of those people who can make that kind of leap, I'm afraid I'm just not. While our lives are often a patchwork quilt of magical coincidences and serendipitous meetings, the thing to remember about a patchwork quilt is that someone has had to sit there and hand-stitch each square in place. And so when folk like me start telling you to just jump, that can cause inordinate pressure and make you feel like a colossal failure if you're thinking, 'But I have a mortgage or rent payment due on the first of every month.' More importantly, the 'jump first' perspective very often comes from a place of immense privilege. It is easy to have faith if you have a financial safety net. When it's just you and the dog (or your equivalent) in your little family set-up, it can feel harder to take those leaps.

While it might be tempting to consult a psycho-geography guru to help figure out if your choice of a new home is going to work with your astrological map (and I do believe that these tools can help when you have the freedom of a blank canvas), the chances are that it's your life circumstances that are going to dictate where you move. It might be determined by a new job for you or your partner; where your family needs to be; where older relatives are situated; where you can afford to live.

Nevertheless, there are likely to be little chips of freedom hidden away in all of this. For example, as the lockdowns of Covid progressed, I came to realise that all the things that had been keeping me rooted to London had vanished. My work had become home-based, my teaching went online, my favourite yoga classes were cancelled, I had completed my PhD and my decree absolute came through. What was I clinging on to in my studio flat on the very edges of the city? I realised that I was now free to follow the summer wind, and it was blowing south-west. All of the cards that determined the shape of my life were in flux, and I knew I was going home.

When you are weighing up the possibilities and the potential, try to look at 'old' information from a different angle. Maybe the role that was once out of reach because it would have involved heavy commuting is now possible from your dream location with a couple of days working from home each week? Perhaps a move to a cheaper area isn't what you had in mind, but could it also bring you closer to a community or a place you could come to love? Is there a path concealed behind a gate wound around with ivy and honeysuckle that you just couldn't see before?

It may be that in the first instance you decide or need to stay where you are, but you can bring what you desire closer nonetheless. If you long for a smallholding, perhaps there's a community garden closer to home where you could test things out? If the sea is what moves you, could you schedule a few day trips or investigate local lakes? If the cultural life of the big city is calling, try streaming theatre or gigs into your front room. Creating the space to satisfy these longings in your world as it is right now will make it more likely that you'll be able to bring your larger vision into existence further down the line.

When I used to walk for more than an hour each morning from locked-down zone five to reach the peacefulness of the woods, I would tell my unconscious mind, 'More of this, please.' As I sat beneath the leaf-filled hornbeams and oak trees, listening to the song thrush that interspersed its song with impersonations of blackbirds and buzzards, I would gaze upwards and think about the sky across which the birds were gliding. Giving yourself a taste of the thing that you really want can help to open up the neural pathways of possibility to get you there. Carve out the space and time to experience the thing that you love on a micro-level to begin to create it in the macro.

TRY THIS: A SEVEN-DAY WITCH BOTTLE FOR LEAVING YOUR HOME (AND MAKING A PERFECT NEW ONE)

In this exercise we are going to be combining three kinds of tried-and-tested old magic to help with the process of leaving one home and making another. First we'll connect with the pre-modern planetary powers, which date to ancient Babylon in the second millennium BCE. At this time, humans looked up to the heavens without the aid of modern telescopes and saw two luminaries (the sun and moon) and five 'wandering stars' moving across the skies – we now know that these were the planets Mercury, Venus, Mars, Jupiter and Saturn.

Our second technique will be to create a 'witch bottle', an idea that dates to the seventeenth century. In our magical past, practitioners and healers would make witch bottles for counter-magic (magic to prevent other spells from working) in the home, using all sorts of 'protective' ingredients such as nails, hair and urine. But don't worry, ours is going to be more sweet-smelling than that!

The third technique is candle magic, a very effective form of spell working. Ever blown out your birthday-cake candles and made a wish? If so, you've been doing candle magic all your life. And remember, if your logical mind is railing at my use of the words 'spell' or 'magic', what we are really doing is using symbols to communicate with our unconscious mind in creating a goal.

When selling or leaving a home, it is important that you complete any unresolved tasks in that space, making peace and reaching an agreement with the spirit of your home that you will let each other go so that you can find a new home and it can find a new family.

We are going to be working with all seven of the pre-modern planets on each of their given days of the week, using the colours associated with each of them. We are also going to be employing an element of sympathetic magic by using items linked to both you and your home. For the purposes of the spell, it is important to link the items to the person or people who are recorded on the official paperwork as owning or renting the property (if you are renting a place, that means you, not your landlord – you really don't want your landlord to sell up and leave you homeless).

You will need:

* An incense charcoal and a censer (see pages 23–4 for how to prepare them)
* Some dried sage or frankincense grains
* A glass jar with a sealable lid, such as a Kilner jar or clean jam jar
* Something to represent your relationship with the property you want to leave or move into. This could be a copy of the first page of the official paperwork – the deeds to the house, the estate agent's brochure, the rental agreement, etc. (But don't use the original!)
* Some coloured threads representing each of the planets (in order) – white, red, orange, purple, green, black, gold or yellow
* Nine dried jasmine flowers (moon)
* Five dried chilis (Mars)
* Eight sprigs of lavender flowers, or eight pinches of dried lavender (Mercury)
* Four cloves (Jupiter)
* Seven dried rose petals or buds (Venus)
* Three sprinkles of dried patchouli leaves (Saturn) or three beech leaves or three sprigs of yew – go out and gather these responsibly. A tip: you will find yew trees in most graveyards
* Six dried orange slices (sun)
* Seven spell candles (small ones) in each of the following colours: white, red, orange, purple, green, black and gold or yellow

* One white candle or taper (to be used to fix each candle to the bottom of the jar)

You can begin this spell on any day, but if you can end it on either a Saturday or Sunday, it would be extra helpful. This is because Saturday is the day of endings (ruled by Saturn) and Sunday is the day of successful endeavours (ruled by the sun). While you are doing the actions for each day, think about how that planet can help you in your endeavour. For example, with Venus being the planet of love, you might ask it to help you and your old home let go of one another with compassion. With Mercury, planet of speed and merchants, you could implore it to help you move as quickly as possible. Or with the moon (not a planet, I know), think about how it can help your intuition work most effectively in negotiating the contracts and therefore staying ahead of the curve. To help you work it out, the days and their associations are as follows:

> Monday – the day of the moon, revealing what is unconscious, intuitive and hidden beneath the surface. Use the white candle and thread, and the jasmine flowers as outlined below.

> Tuesday – the day of Mars, planet of protection, boundary setting and confidence. Use the red thread, the red candle and the dried chilis.

> Wednesday – the day of Mercury, planet of speed, selling and communication. Use the orange candle and thread, and the lavender.

> Thursday – the day of Jupiter, planet of expansion and wealth. Use the purple candle and thread, and the cloves.

Friday – the day of Venus, planet of love, friendship and harmony. Use the green candle and thread, and the rose petals or buds.

Saturday – the day of Saturn, planet of endings, grounding and a sense of belonging. Use the black candle and thread, and the sprigs of yew or beech or the patchouli leaves.

Sunday – the day of Sol, the sun, which rules over success, sovereignty and health. Use the yellow or gold thread and candle, and the dried orange pieces or slices.

While you carry out the following actions, I invite you to think of yourself in your new home, with all your loved ones inside happy, healthy and safe. Think of your old home with new occupants, likewise healthy, happy and fulfilled. It needs to be a compelling image, as this will seep into the spell as you hold it in mind, but let yourself fall into a naturally playful state if you can. Magic works best when you are relaxed, having a bit of fun and enjoying what you are doing.

Begin by cleansing your current home by burning either some sage leaves or frankincense on an incense charcoal. Walk in an anti-clockwise direction, to send out any residual negativity. When you are done with the sacred smoke, open all the windows to let it out.

Next, make sure the jar is clean and dry. Take your photocopy of the official document and on it write a line or two connected to how that day's planet will help you – for example, on a Friday, you might write, 'I release you with love.' Picture it happening quickly, with surprising speed and a requisite whoosh. If you already have a new home in mind, you can take the picture of that property instead and write 'bought with love' on the back (or whatever is appropriate for today's planet).

Next, take your matching candle and carve it with the name of your home; add the word 'sold' (or 'bought' for the new home) and your initials. Fix the candle inside the jar using some of the white taper wax on the bottom, then light it while picturing the speed and ease with which your home will sell or you'll rent or buy the new place. Allow the candle to burn all the way down. Lastly, measure out the herbs for the day and put them in a separate dish or bowl for now. (You will add them to the jar at the end of the spellcasting, on the last day.) Keep the deed or image with the jar and the herbs until tomorrow.

Over the next six days, gather the ingredients for the planet in question and repeat the instructions above.

On the last day, take the last candle and carve on it as before. Then fold up the paper you've been using, tying it with the threads as you picture closing the door on your old home for the last time. Send it some love as you go and imagine opening up the new.

Measure out the last herb and then add all the herbs to the jar, one at a time, picturing that end result as you do so. Add your paper document to the jar and, this time, seal the lid. Say the words, 'As I do will it with love, so mote it be.' Then, using some taper wax, attach the last candle to the lid of the sealed jar. You are using it to charge up the entire seven days' worth of spell. Light the candle and carefully let it burn out, keeping an eye on it as it does.

The final piece of the magic is to find somewhere safe and secure to hide the jar – preferably near the entrance to your current home. That might mean tucking it in a cupboard or boot store just inside your entranceway or burying it in the ground outside your front door. You might have to get creative here with a large pot plant if you live in an apartment.

In the coming days and weeks, do everything you can to work positively towards selling your home in the material world – work with the estate agents to give them what they need, keep your home loved and clean while you are in it, and make sure it is tidy and smelling sweet when people come to view it.

When I was trying to sell my place, things moved with surprising speed once I created this witch bottle for finding the perfect new home.

DISEMBARKING: STARTING AGAIN MAY TAKE TIME

For the next few days, they journeyed onward out of the forest and onto the moors, following their animal companions. They walked until their feet were sore and their backs ached. At night, they camped and huddled together around a small fire, more to feel connected than for the warmth.

'How will we ever find a new home?' Elizabeth whispered to Sam, hoping not to wake Puck and worry him.

'We must keep following the other animals,' said Sam, 'and have faith there will be a place for us.'

So they walked onward through the next day, and the day after, and the day after that, until eventually they came to the top of a high hill that looked down over a wide valley. The valley was filled with verdant trees, and there was not a single person in sight, not a road, only the wide valley filled with trees and a clean river that meandered on through.

'There,' said Sam. 'Down there we will find our home.'

They made their way down the hillside, in among the boulders of granite that had been thrown out by the mountains and journeyed long before the trees sprang up between them. The forest was dense and thick, full of moss and lichen, but the sunlight was dappled green among the leaves. *The squirrels undulated across the branches and the wild ponies grazed in the patches of grass that lay between the great trunks.*

'Here is the place of my song-dream,' said Sam. 'Where the wild god still roams. Here we can live free.'

It was Puck who found the perfect spot. 'Over there,' he said, pointing to a clearing. 'Between the two beech trees and the sycamores.'

They made their new home in the curve of the river and, when they lay down to sleep at night, they heard the river gurgling by, and the owls hooting across the valley, and they lay undisturbed. By day, they explored the new forest, by night they rested beneath its limbs, and in time they began to forget that they'd ever known anywhere different.

Hurrah! You've moved home, you've found your tribe, you've relocated yourself in space and time. But what now? It's likely that you are a little 'all at sea'. We have been sold the idea of a 'happy ending' though all of our cultural references – from fairy tales to Hollywood films – and have come to expect that life will be tied up with a bow once we've taken the plunge and made that move (or started that new relationship, job or any other life change you care to name). However, you may well have found in life so far that the prince very quickly turns into a slightly creased human being, and that the castle you have gone to live in turns out to be a normal house that needs fixing and maintaining, with a lot of work to keep it tidy. If you are feeling a sense of despondency because it isn't quite the ending you were hoping for, do not despair. As John Lennon (and a million other sources on the internet) once said, 'Everything will be OK in the end. If it's not OK, it's not the end.'

After I made my move out of the city to a more rural location, there were nights when I would wake up, bolt upright, and wonder what on earth I had done. With such a huge decision, it's only natural that you should have moments of doubt. With that in mind, there are two final thoughts I would like to leave you with. The first is that we tend to regret the things we haven't done more than the things we have tried. And the second is to remind you of those four points of connectivity – those competencies, opportunities, motivations and perceptions. Settling into a new place will take time and concerted effort to build up those fresh connections, friends and projects that make it feel like your safe place. Set the ball rolling with this ritual of welcome in your new home.

TRY THIS: AN INCENSE TO CLEANSE YOUR NEW HOME AND WELCOME YOU IN

Over the centuries, humans have burned incenses to make offerings to the deities they worship and to cleanse spaces of energy, to welcome in love, friendship or abundance. We are going to create an incense that is multi-functioning: it does a little of all of this.

One of the first magical workings any witch will do when moving into a new home is to energetically cleanse the space of any 'leftovers' from whoever lived there before, and also to make a little offering to the spirit of this new place to help them bond with it.

As well as using that cleansing and welcoming incense, we are going to create an altar or meditative space to the *genius loci* or the *lar familiaris* of your home. In an ancient Roman home these were not only the household gods; they also looked out for the treasured possessions of that home.

To burn loose incense, you will need a roll of charcoal discs and a censer (see page 23 for my homemade mug version).

Fill up the censer with earth from your local area as an additional link to your home – you can stop when you're around two centimetres below the brim. Later you will place the lit charcoal disc on top of this and the earth will prevent the mug from getting too hot.

But first, let's make an incense and then get our home and altar in order.

For the incense you will need:

* A pestle and mortar (or similar) to grind the herbs into tiny pieces or powder, as large chunks of herb in an incense can sometimes smell bitter
* One teaspoon of dried sage (for cleansing)
* One teaspoon of lavender (for happiness)
* One teaspoon of rose petals (for love)
* Two bay leaves scrunched up into small pieces (for health and healing)
* Two cloves (for abundance)
* Two teaspoons of frankincense resin
* Two teaspoons of myrrh resin
* Six drops of rose essential oil

Begin by grinding the herbs in the pestle and mortar, then add the frankincense and myrrh resin, and finally the essential oil. Any leftovers can be kept in an airtight jar.

For the ritual, you will need:

* A flat space in your home on which to create an altar: this could be a cleared windowsill, bookshelf or table
* An altar cloth in your favourite colour
* A white candle – a tea light in a glass for safe burning works well
* A bell or glass (though this isn't essential)
* A small vase with some greenery or flowers gathered from your garden or local area – remember to leave some for the insects, animals and other humans

* A collection of special items that represent home, family and loved ones, living or deceased

Begin by cleaning your home from top to toe. This is an important part of the ritual as the idea is to completely cleanse the space both physically and energetically before you build your household altar. If you can do each room in turn, moving in an anti-clockwise direction, this will make it extra witchy, as we always banish things in this *widdershins* way. Pay particular attention to any doors leading in or out of your home, the kitchen (or hearth) of your home, as well as the area where you are going to place your altar. Open all the windows to give the place a really good airing.

Once everywhere is clean, go around your home, again in a widdershins direction, to cleanse the energy by sounding the bell, gently striking your glass or clapping your hands. Sound cleansing has been used for thousands of years around the globe – think of wind chimes or gongs. Have some fun with it, adding in some pan banging, involving other members of your household and enjoy yourselves. There is nothing quite so good for the energy of the home as laughter.

Pay particular attention to corners, darkened spaces or hidden parts where energy might have gathered for a while. If you'd like to add some words to your bellringing, pot-clanging, clapping ceremony, you can say:

> Spirits who have gathered here over time, we
>   release you with love.
> Energies who have stayed here and
>   become stuck,
> We release you and send you on your way
>   with love.

Go out into the world with our love.
We release you.

When you have had a good old time making a bit of noise,
gather together in the room where the altar will be. Place
the cloth on the altar and spend some time arranging on it
the items that represent your intention to make your home a
loving, healthy and happy one. Place the flowers and white
candle on there too. Light the candle and say:

> Spirit of this place,
> Ancestors of our line,
> We welcome you into this place.
> May you find peace here.
> May you find love here.
> And bless us with your presence.

Light your charcoal disc and, using kitchen tongs to avoid
burns, place it on top of the earth in the censer. It is also a
good idea to keep a window open for ventilation and keep
your smalls – children, non-human animals and birds – away
from the incense smoke. The disc will spark as it takes light.

When the charcoal has turned grey, it is ready. Take a
small pinch of the incense and place it atop the charcoal. As
the smoke starts to curl upwards, say:

> *Lar familiaris*, we welcome you into our home.
> May you find rest here with us.
> May you find love here with us.
> May you find happiness here with us.
> May you find prosperity here with us.
> *May you find peacefulness here with us.*

If you can carry the censer safely and without burning your-selves or your lovely new home, take it into each room in a *deosil* or clockwise direction and repeat the words of welcome. When you have completed your circuit, celebrate and ground yourselves by sharing a meal together.

Over the coming weeks and months, keep adding new items to your altar space while taking away things you no longer feel the need to work with. This way, the energy will not become 'stuck'. We are not casting this space in amber – we want it to remain 'living' as the seasons change and your life and home change with them.

In our next season and on the final segment of our journey, we are moving onwards through the woods to autumn to consider how we might approach the later-stage life changes of menopause and self-actualisation – the process of becoming everything you are capable of being so that you can live a more satisfying life, and one that encompasses all you love best.

PART FOUR
AUTUMN IN THE WOODS

Perhaps they say: 'One hour
More, and we dance among the golden sheaves . . .
Make haste, O slack gale, to the looked-for land!'
My trees are not in flower,
I have no bower,
And gusty creaks my tower,
And lonesome, very lonesome, is my strand.

Christina Rossetti

THEMES: Maturing, coming into your power
PLANET: Jupiter
ELEMENT: Water
DIRECTION: West
TIME OF DAY: Evening

Autumn in the woods speaks to the senses. The eyes feast on the gold, yellow and red that begin to appear at the outer edges of the leaves, creeping inwards with the retreating sap. This is the season of the stag rutting, of the leaves starting to crackle underfoot. The woods resound to the football rattle of the jay and the mocking cackle of the crow. The horse chestnut has turned early this year, weakened by a virus, while the oaks take their time in their yellowing before turning golden. The susurration, so gentle in summer when the canopy was supple and green, now takes on a crepitating quality. Each gust loosens a few more dry leaves, until the litter at our feet swishes around us as we walk. Those dead leaves will remain in evidence long into the next year, moistened by each rainfall, until eventually they become a new layer of topsoil. The beech trees defy this pattern, frequently holding on to their leaves throughout the winter storms, a trait known as marcescence, from the Latin, *marcescere*, to fade. The old foliage will remain in place until the new spring leaves push through and dislodge it.

Autumn is ruled by the planet Jupiter, representing the expansive benevolence of middle age, where (allegedly) we have reached a point where we can be comfortable. Life is rarely as simple as that, however. While in nature the autumn trees are heavy with generous berries and fruit – ruby hawthorn, the indigo elder and the brilliant scarlet of the rowan – for too many of us there is scarcity while wealth is hoarded and unevenly distributed across our societies. Instead, at this time of life, we may want or need to reassess our values and our expectations. Is it riches we want or richness of experience?

Autumn returns us to a place of balance between the light that still holds and the coming darkness, if only for a fleeting moment. In the woods, the evenings are drawing in; the earth smells loamy and, nestled in the undergrowth, mushrooms – there is decay and there is new possibility side-by-side. In our life changes, we likewise turn our attention to themes associated with a sense of maturing – the coming of age, menopause and self-actualisation, where we'll ground ourselves in what fulfils and nourishes us in abundance.

CHAPTER SEVEN
THE JOURNEY OF EMBRACING MENOPAUSE

Yet hope again elastic springs,
Unconquered, though she fell;
Still buoyant are her golden wings,
Still strong to bear us well.

Charlotte Brontë

TAROT CARD: Nine of Swords

Menstruation can be a bit of a loaded topic. So many of us spend our lives cursing the inconvenience or discomfort. At worst the terms some use to describe it are insulting and malign – 'the curse', 'shark week', 'carrie', 'on the rag', 'the crimson tide' and more – or euphemisms that add an air of the mysterious. It's no wonder that some of us are feeling the need to reclaim this natural process from the far-flung insults.

More recently, people have been looking to other cultures around the world, for ways of celebrating a first period or menarche (from the Latin *mensis* or month, which was derived from the Greek *mene* for moon, coupled with the ancient Greek philosophical term established by Aristotle, *archéē*, or originating source.) For example, in some southern Indian communities, the first period is welcomed through *Ritusuddi*, when the girl receives gifts and her first sari, while, in Japan, the family shares a celebratory meal of *sekihan* – sticky rice and adzuki beans, their red colour symbolising the first period and the happiness it brings as a sign of growing up. Yet we aren't so good at celebrating the last period, let alone the whimsical and capricious menses of perimenopause – that time of transition prior to menopause. Of course, this has very practical reasons. We don't know at the time that a menstrual period will be the last, since menopause is only medically marked twelve months after the last period, but in recent years, women who identify as pagan, or who have decided to take a more feminist approach to their spiritual lives, have started to create celebratory rituals connected to the menopause or this time of 'croning'.

Fed up with the idea that 'women of a certain age' become invisible and past their sell-by date just because they can no longer conceive without medical intervention, they are reclaiming the pejorative language that is often used to describe older women – 'hag', 'crone', 'hellcat', 'virago', 'carline', 'shrew' or, my personal favourite, 'witch' – and turning the concept on its head. You may have seen these people in your own community. Perhaps they have dyed their hair in brilliant colours or chosen clothes that make you stop and stare. Or perhaps there's something about them that's unexpected, opinionated, celebratory, rebellious even. They are entering into their third age of life, have gone through a second Saturn Return (yes, you read that right, there's a second one – gulp) and don't feel that anyone is entitled to tell them what to do any more. Fabulous.

In the patriarchal model, those of us who have gone beyond child-bearing ability are only useful as carers (either for the sick, the young, or the elderly), but in the croning model of life this is a new beginning, and it inevitably brings with it some of those existential questions we sometimes face in life. For example, how can we live well in this autumn of our experience? How can we ride this wave of upheaval that can be shattering, but that is also a time of reinvention and reimagining? How can we create a different kind of fertile base from which to grow? But first, let's consider what menopause is and how it can affect so many of us.

PREPARING FOR THE JOURNEY: UNDERSTANDING MENOPAUSE

Years passed in the woodland, and the imperfect goddess and her woodsman did their best in bringing up Puck to be a thoughtful, considerate and kind person. He was intensely fair-minded, and often brought home wounded animals that he found in the forest, caring for them until they were well again and could go on their way. Soon Puck became known in the locality, and people would bring him wounded creatures, knowing that he would nurse them back to health.

But, as time passed, Elizabeth found her love of life seemed to leave her a little. Her body no longer seemed supple and lithe. She felt tired, and ached, even though her monthly courses seemed to have stopped. She wondered what the cause might be. While Elizabeth loved her family dearly, there were times when she felt alone and she longed for the company of other women to talk to. She wondered if Margaret was still to be found deep in the woods, or would she have long since vanished?

Speak about menopause in our parents' generation and it was often behind a hand, with a wink or lots of gesticulations as people whispered about 'the change' as if they might explode if they said it too loud. As a consequence, it's one of those areas that many of us have been ill-informed about over the years. And that's before we even get to the confusion that can arise over language, gender identity and what constitutes womanhood. So, for the sake of starting off as we mean to go on, let's begin by agreeing a few definitions. Throughout this chapter I will be non-gendered in my use of pronouns, as menopause can be experienced by a whole range of people who menstruate.

While menopause itself is medically defined as the time twelve months after a person last menstruated, it's the symptoms of peri-menopause that give us so much grief, discomfort and disruption. Perimenopause can last for an indeterminate amount of time, which is why it's so hard to navigate: there is no easily defined beginning and end point. Post-menopause is used to describe people who have stopped menstruating. It's tempting to think of this as 'coming out the other side'.

One tip for this chapter is to exercise caution when consult-ing online sources of information about this topic, as there is a frightening amount of misinformation and insensitivity out there. In my chapter notes at the end of the book, you'll find a range of reliable resources that you might find helpful. These have all been recommended to me and road-tested by colleagues who are part of a menopause support allyship group in my workplace. We meet regularly and talk through any confusing information we have encountered, share thoughts on what has been helpful and have a lot of laughs along the way. One of the challenges of losing my mother to cancer in my thirties is that I didn't have her to turn to for advice and support when I started experiencing symptoms. It's my familial sisters and this allyship group who have helped me to fill that gap, so do cast your net widely to see who in your life might be able to help support you through this process. If you are intending to seek medical support, especially around the area of HRT, it helps if you are well informed before you visit your GP so that you can clearly advocate for what you want and need. Remember also: you are the expert on how your body feels and the range of unusual things that might be occurring.

We're going to begin by reminding ourselves that this is not an issue that only affects women of a certain age. If you identify as male and have never menstruated but know someone who has – either a friend, partner, spouse, sibling or parent – this will affect you too. This can be a bewildering time for any person, but if they have a supportive and open supporter or partner to help with navigating this transition, it can go a long way. We also need to get over the idea that this only happens later in life – all sorts of medical conditions and treatments can cause someone to experience menopause at an early age, with all the life-changing implications this brings for their health and fertility.

NHS England suggests there are around 13 million people who are currently peri- or menopausal in the UK – around a third of the entire UK female population. That's a lot of people who have been failed by poor information, poor access to advice and treatment, and poor support. So, let's start having a look at some of the symptoms and areas of misinformation, so we can start to navigate a clear path.

READING THE MAP: SYMPTOMS TO LOOK OUT FOR

Elizabeth knew that she must seek out the company of her own kind, but how was she to begin? Then she remembered there had been women who had passed by over the years – the mother of one of Puck's friends, the wife of one of Sam's companions. One of the women who had brought Puck a wounded blackbird to care for.

'Why is it,' Elizabeth thought to herself, 'that all of these women are present, but I only ever see them in the context of their menfolk? Why should they be only the mother of . . . or the wife of . . .'

And so, Elizabeth decided that she would change this.

The range of symptoms you might be experiencing if you are menopausal or perimenopausal are surprisingly vast. But during a recent gathering of my menopause support champions, we compared notes and there were quite a few exclamations of surprise. 'I had no idea itching was one of the symptoms,' one colleague told me.

Some of the better-known ones include heavy or irregular periods, insomnia, brain fog, mood swings, anxiety, hot flushes and break-outs of acne or dry skin (or both). However, there are some very helpful apps out there, such as The Balance App, which can help you learn about the wide-ranging and disparate indications you might be enduring. You can also use this app to track the symptoms you are experiencing and when, helping you to build a case as to why you need to be given access to treatment. Too often women have been prescribed anti-depressants, or given treatment such as cognitive behavioural therapy when the cacophony of symptoms they are experiencing can be explained by the drop in oestrogen, testosterone and progesterone levels that comes during this transition. As the Menopause Charity (an organisation whose name says it all) states:

> As life expectancy has increased, you can expect to be post-menopausal for at least one third of your life. This is why it's important to think of the menopause as a long-term female hormone deficiency. Like any other deficiency, this is associated with several health risks.

These health risks include osteoporosis, cardio-vascular disease, diabetes, dementia, clinical depression and a range of other illnesses, including asthma, kidney disease, irritable bowel syndrome and osteoarthritis. The good news, however, is that the likelihood of many of these can be reduced with hormone replacement therapy, often known as HRT – for too long an enormous elephant in the room.

The HRT elephant comes with several accompanying mythologies, and it can be quite overwhelming when you try to find a clear path through these trees. I would encourage you to read widely on this topic, and reach your own conclusions. But let's have a look at some of the myths and where they come from.

First myth: that HRT only prolongs the menopausal process by 'putting it off until later'. According to the Menopause Charity, however:

> HRT simply treats the symptoms of the menopause. If you experience menopause symptoms when you stop taking it, this isn't a result of taking hormones. You would still have been having the same symptoms even if you'd never taken HRT.

Second myth: that HRT causes breast cancer. This was put about following some very unhelpful headlines connected to a controversial piece of research called The Women's Health Initiative, carried out in America between 1993 and around 2007.

This one is quite a biggie in terms of unhelpful information doing the rounds and it is still hard to find sources that marry up, as different findings were published at different stages of the research. The study was intended to look at women taking oestrogen-only HRT and others taking a combined oestrogen and progesterone HRT, and to compare both groups with women taking a placebo. However, various questions arose about the study's validity; the oestrogen-only part of the study was halted early, due to safety concerns; and some of the 'results' were also published early, which led to them being skewed, but cited as if they were fact in the press. This had a devastating effect on women's health. Some estimates are that 50 per cent of women stopped taking HRT overnight. According to Dr Louise Newson, a GP and renowned menopause expert:

> The results of this study were leaked to the press early, before they had been properly analysed. The subsequent

sub-analysis of this study showed that women taking HRT are healthier and have less diseases than those women not taking HRT.

Sadly, while the study included some helpful information, the misinformation has remained prevalent, even though subsequent studies have shown that the risk of breast cancer while taking combined HRT is much less than initially reported: it equates to four extra cases per thousand women after five years, a risk less than that caused by smoking ten cigarettes a day, alcohol and obesity.

The guidelines from the National Institute for Health and Care Excellence (NICE), a body that decides what drugs and treatments are available in the UK, now advise HRT as the best form of treatment for hormone deficiency, with all those associated health risks, but somehow that message is still not getting through to patients and even to doctors. This leaves an awful lot of women potentially suffering completely unnecessary ill effects.

Many people explore (and spend a lot of money on) 'natural remedies', but that doesn't mean these are safer or more effective than prescribed HRT. The natural remedies often contain very little oestrogen, and are not necessarily the right type of hormone for the human body.

If you are suffering from the effects of hormone deficiency, the best thing you can do for yourself is begin a research journey that's specific to you. As a starting point, I would particularly recommend Dr Louise Newson's Balance website and the Menopause Charity, plus the Daisy Network for anyone in need of support with premature ovarian insufficiency, also known as premature menopause. Once you have armed yourself with the knowledge you need, do then seek out your menopause or women's health specialist through your surgery. You may need to be persistent, but also remember that the choice is yours. It's your body.

TRY THIS: BATH SALTS TO STAVE OFF THE MEAN REDS

When I used to run a tiny business making traditional soaps and bath salts, there was one secret recipe people repeatedly asked me to share: my formula for these bath salts, for those days when you feel afraid, sweat like hell and are convinced that something bad is just around the corner. Up until now I have never shared it with anyone, but if you're trying to find your way through the woods of your (peri)menopause, you're going to want to administer as much self-care as you can. So I think it's time to break the seal on the top-secret vault.

Obviously, this recipe comes with the usual caveats around ideas of 'healing'. It's not a miracle cure. If you are taking medication, you'll still need to do so, but a bath containing these salts will feel like a warm hug when you most need one. Feel free to use artistic licence when it comes to what kind of salt to use – if you want to add an extra layer of Venus-inspired love, for example, then use some Himalayan pink salt instead. I quite like the contrast of the different colours, but if you can't get this, regular sea salt is fine. This recipe will make enough bath salts for several sessions, so store them in an airtight jar out of direct sunlight for another day.

You will need:

* One cup of coarse-grained sea salt
* Three cups of fine-grained sea salt
* One cup of Epsom salts
* Half a cup of dried rose petals – optional, but they look beautiful in the bath
* Seven drops of rose essential oil

* Seven drops of clary sage essential oil, though this comes with a warning: if there is any chance you might be pregnant, consult a medical practitioner before using it
* Seven drops of rose geranium essential oil

Take a large mixing bowl and add the sea salt (both coarse and fine) with the Epsom salts. Epsom salts contain magnesium, which is why they are so good for muscle aches. Mix the salts with your hand or a spoon until they are evenly distributed. While you are mixing, think calming thoughts of your most relaxed version of you, lying back in a bath in a candle-lit bathroom.

Now add the essential oils, carefully counting the seven drops of each one (see page 118 for the significance of the number seven). Mix them in thoroughly, as if you were rubbing butter into flour – you want a nice even distribution. Finally, add the rose petals if you are using them.

The bath salts will be ready to use straight away, so draw a nice warm bath and drop in a couple of tablespoons of the salts, letting them dissolve in the water.

A tip about storage: let the salts dry out overnight before you seal them into an airtight jar. I once had an impressive performance of exploding bath salts as I hadn't let the oils dry out first and they began to ferment in the bottle. Ahem.

THE MENOPAUSE IN NATURE

The next time that Puck was visited by one of his friends, Elizabeth asked him to pass a note to his mother. In it, she expressed a wish to meet and be friendly and, much to her delight, the next day, Puck's friend's mother appeared outside their door.

'Rose,' she said. 'My name is Rose, and I am very happy to meet you.' Rose was of a similar age, and soon she and Elizabeth were meeting every week, keeping each other company and comparing notes on their years as women of the world. Elizabeth had a warm feeling each time she thought about her new friend, and then other women started to join them for their regular gatherings. In time, a group of women had formed, all of a similar age or older.

Elizabeth had got her wish, and had a circle of women around her.

With a heading such as 'The Menopause in Nature', it's fitting to remind ourselves that we are also part of the natural world – it's not a separate entity. And so, looking at this wider perspective might help us to put our experiences in context. Especially when we might ask why, if the menopause has such devastating health effects, we have to make this transition. Looking at the other-than-human animal kingdom can offer us some clues.

According to several academic studies, menopause does occur in other species, but in different forms to humans. In gorillas in captivity, for example, a menopause is observed, but gorillas don't tend to live for very long after they cease to be fertile. Biological menopause in the way that humans experience it has only been observed in orcas and pilot whales, but the reason this occurs is one of those ways in which nature shows us just how fascinating she can be.

With orcas, just as with humans, the young of the species take many years to mature – indeed, some males may always remain dependent on their mothers for food. Matriarchal orcas are thought to share 90 per cent of the food they catch, as opposed to the 40 per cent that adult males share. In addition, orcas live in a matrilineal society: their family groups, or pods, are led by the oldest female in the family, who takes responsibility for teaching the younger members of the pod how to fish. So you can see how the idea that a post-menopausal matriarch might lose her usefulness would be ludicrous.

Orcas and humans share the fact of a long life after our fertile days are over and, contrary to what our grandparents' generation might have been told, our usefulness after this change is not depleted in any way. As Dr Kirtly Parker Jones at the University of Utah suggests, 'post-menopausal women are the civilising force of society', both in human terms and in the non-human animal kingdom.

TRY THIS: JOURNALING FOR YOUR MENTAL HEALTH AND MENOPAUSE

One of the biggest challenges we can face when navigating the sometimes bewildering path through menopause or hormone deficiency is the hit that our mental health can take, especially when we feel as if our body is out of control or no longer familiar to us. At the beginning of this chapter I listed the tarot card for menopause as the Nine of Swords: it depicts a woman sitting up in bed, holding her head in her hands. It can suggest anxiety, sleeplessness, mental health challenges, insomnia and migraines, all of which are symptoms of (peri)menopause. It also hints at the need to find ways to cope with life's challenges that don't involve self-medicating with drugs, alcohol, shopping, sex, gambling or any of the other behaviours associated with addictions. Yet when reversed (or in other words, pulled from the pack upside down), the card can also indicate the light at the end of the tree-lined tunnel – you may be coming out of that period of sleepless nights and finding a renewed sense of peace.

When you face such challenges, turning to your journal can be a helpful activity. Spending just thirty minutes or so regrouping can do you the world of good, especially if you are feeling isolated, as if you are the only person in your area of the woods today. This exercise is designed to help guide you in three things. Firstly, what support does your inner self, or unconscious mind, feel that it needs right now? Secondly, who do you know who can help you with that? And thirdly, how might you support yourself with that?

Spend some time with your journal in a quiet place that allows for reflection and note down some answers to the following questions. You can write as much or as little as you like. If it's an image that comes to mind instead, note that down or even draw the picture you're holding in mind.

- Who did you look up to when you were younger?
- What did you admire about them?
- Who do you know now who displays those traits?
- Think of someone in your life who has been nurturing. How did they show you love and support?
- Could you reach out to them now?
- How can you respond to yourself in the way they would have done?
- What would you say if a friend approached you with the feelings or thoughts that you are experiencing?

EMBARKING: YOUR SECOND SATURN RETURN AND POSITIVE MENOPAUSE ARCHETYPES

At long last, Elizabeth had people she could ask advice from. Although it was many years since she had last seen Margaret, or felt the presence of her mother around her, she knew that both were with her in the spirit of the circle of women.

This did not diminish her love of Sam and Puck. If anything, it strengthened it as she now felt she was carried in the arms of her beloved

*women. They shared their experiences of life willingly and freely, and
so learning from them became as natural to Elizabeth as running water.
Looking around at the faces of the circle, seeing the laughter lines around
the eyes of the women, and the creased cheeks and grey hairs starting
to show in some, while dominating in others, Elizabeth knew she was
in the unique position of being unafraid of getting older. How could she
fear something, when she could see all around her what fabulous lives
her circle of friends were living?*

In witches' circles we refer to the period in your late twenties as your
'Saturn Return'. This is when the planet Saturn – usually associated
with foundations, stability and endings – completes its twenty-
eight-year cycle around our sun and comes back to the position it
was in at your birth, thereby encouraging you to question all that
you once thought was stable, logical and known. Does any of this
sound familiar?

I hate to be the bearer of bad news, but all this happens again
another twenty-eight years later. While around the age of twenty-
eight you might have had a career change or your first child or
perhaps a change of location, your second Saturn Return, when
you are in your mid-fifties, might coincide with that child leaving
home or perhaps spell the ending of a significant relationship or
mark the loss of a parent. In fact, you could be making your way
through any of the previous chapters of this book up until this one.
And of course this second Saturn Return usually also coincides
with (peri)menopause.

All of this change or questioning can suddenly mean that you
feel untethered, lost in the woods. Just at the point at which you
expected to have figured out how life works, you find yourself bewil-
dered and wondering what on earth has gone wrong. Fortunately,
there are some very important archetypes that you can turn to at
this time. While each person's truth is different and individual to

them, what drew me in to modern paganism was a spiritual practice that venerates femininity, instead of telling me I was unclean just because I menstruated, or that I was the weaker sex, subservient to men.

The Wiccan triple goddess has her beginnings in the female archetypes prevalent in the ancient world. Often these were lunar deities, goddesses carrying with them the threefold aspects that are associated with the moon: the waxing or growing moon; the full moon when it reaches its zenith; and the waning moon, growing smaller. In ancient Greece, there was Hecate, the goddess of three aspects who guarded the crossroads – particularly those where three roads meet – and held her lantern aloft to light the way, and her sister goddess, Artemis, who hunted the forest by day or by moonlight. Then from Italy there was Diana and her daughter Aradia, considered to be the mother of all *strega*, or witches. Around the world there are countless more besides: Mama Killa in Incan mythology, Chang Xi of the twelve moons in Chinese culture, Bastet in ancient Egypt. It is these lunar archetypes with whom we might most obviously connect menstruation, and thus menopause. For recent proponents of the pagan faiths, these lunar goddesses also present a very neat archetype for representing the stages of someone who identifies as a woman's wider life – as maiden, mother and crone.

If we expand this thinking further, each one of the trio of archetypes – maiden, mother and crone – can be associated with goddesses from lots of different pantheons. For example, the maiden goddesses include Persephone, Artemis, Mary, Vesta and Minerva and the mother goddesses include Mut, Demeter, Gaia, Lakshmi, Durga, and Hathor. But what about the crones?

Perhaps best known is Baba Yaga, the Slavic ogress who steals and eats children; in Italy we have the old witch La Befana, who delivers presents on Christmas Eve; and then there is my personal favourite, the Cailleach, a Celtic goddess associated with Ireland, Scotland, and the Isle of Man, and known as the Hag of Winter. Associated with storms and thunder, the Cailleach created the Scottish mountains when she strode across the land, dropping rocks from her wicker basket. In some stories she created the earth with her hammer, shaping all of the hills and the valleys, while, in Ireland, the rulers of the land had to seek the approval of the Cailleach before they could take office. In Manx tradition, the Cailleach spends half the year in youth in the spring and summer months and half in the old age of the autumn and winter. In her youthful aspect she is Brigid, the goddess associated with Imbolc or Candlemas, while in winter she returns to her cronehood. While in some traditions cronehood is associated with fear, and ill-wishing, she also carries with her the wisdom of her years.

Yet while the stories of goddesses such as the Cailleach are rich in meaning and carry a more hopeful truth of positive role models at this time of upheaval, there are some obvious drawbacks to the triple moon goddess figure of the maiden-mother-crone. For a start, it works on the assumption that all people who identify as women have these three aspects to their lives, defining us by our relationship to men – untouched by the male gaze, the mother of their children and beyond child-bearing age and therefore interest. It also makes many assumptions about when a person might be experiencing these changes and presumes that there are only these three core defin-itions of self to be experienced, full stop. Nevertheless, even if the idea of maidenhood, motherhood and croning leaves you cold, it is at least the first stirrings of a acceptance of the need for divine feminine archetypes at all. And since we form our concepts of deity by what we need them to reflect, and since there are a vast number of preconceived divine feminine archetypes in the world – and an infinite number more who are yet to be discovered or created – the spiritual world is our oyster. We can define and discover our own goddesses, feminine archetypes and deities, connecting with those with whom we most identify when we need them.

TRY THIS: CONNECTING TO THE DIVINE FEMININE FOR (PERI)MENOPAUSE INSPIRATION

With my Wiccan priestess hat on, I teach a series of workshops that I call 'Meeting the Gods'. In these sessions, we focus on themed archetypes or deities, looking at how to connect and work with them, whether spring gods, lunar gods or deities of death and the underworld. One of the most common questions that comes up in these classes is how to discover and foster a relationship with a specific deity. In short, forming a relationship with a divine being is very much like forming one with a human one – it takes time and a little effort to ensure that you are each clear on what you want to get out of it, and you don't have to rush in and commit a lifetime to someone without testing the waters a little first. We don't form relationships with humans to be completely one-sided (well, hopefully we don't) and the same goes for working in relationship with a deity, which can be hugely rewarding.

The beauty of working in a pantheistic universe is that there are countless archetypes for us to work with throughout our lives, and which can reflect what is going on for us at a specific time. If you are struggling with adapting to this new phase of life, identifying and working with a patron deity for the (peri)menopause can be an empowering and enlightening experience. To find an archetype you want to work with, you have to keep your ears open and your eyes peeled. It's a process of watching for signs and signals and reading the landscape around you. Deities are often accompanied by non-human animal companions, so if your time in nature is suddenly inundated by a particular animal, and if it feels unusual, it may be a sign that a particular divine presence is near and making its presence known. For example, Cailleach Beara is sometimes accompanied by deer, wolves, herons or ravens, while crows often accompany Hecate. I might see crows frequently; however, on one occasion I did take it as a sign of unusual activity when a crow tried to land on my head. That was a signal something was afoot, so I started looking into Hecate to see if she was my 'fit'.

At this point, you'll need a combination of two things: intuition and research. Consider both what you are drawn to and then begin to learn some of the stories of the gods, to get a 'feel' for their personality and how that might work along-side your own. Incidentally, if you are not warming to any of the 'crone' archetypes I have mentioned so far, it's worth remembering they also come with a heavy dose of warrior in them, so they are no shrinking violets.

This exercise is intended to help you with the intuition part of the work, using creative visualisation. It's something we have done with mindfulness exercises already, but I will be asking you to bring in your imagination too.

As ever, we begin with taking yourself off to somewhere safe and quiet where you won't be disturbed. Out in nature would be extra special, but you could also do this at home, on a balcony or in the garden. Perhaps put on relaxing music in the background – something without words, as that would hook you in. Recordings of nature sounds may be a good option, or you may prefer classical music. You want to be able to unwind completely.

Start to focus in on your breath, allowing your body to unclench and breathe at its own pace. Try to deepen your breathing, breathing in for a count of four, holding for four and breathing out for four; then pause for a count of four before the next in-breath. This is known as 'box breathing' and is designed to help calm your nervous system.

When you have unfurled fully, start to allow your awareness to spread out beyond your self into the space around you, and then further still, questing to see if you can sense an awareness or presence. If that feels too abstract, imagine approaching a temple from a short distance away. Perhaps you have floated across a great lake on a boat, trailed your hand in the water and touched the fallen autumn leaves that were floating on the surface. Now you have pulled the boat onto the shore. There's a cool breeze blowing around you as you take in your surroundings. The island is aflame with trees in their full autumn colours, with the leaves showing every shade from gold to red. Perhaps there is a gentle breeze moving the leaves along the surface of the ground, calling you onwards to a temple just ahead of you. You feel safe and completely at home, as if you have been here a thousand times before.

As you approach the temple, you can see an altar in the courtyard, which is placed in front of a large statue. You approach the altar and notice on it candles flickering inside a lantern, and a great censer with a bowl of incense. As you bow your head in reverence and prayer, you take a pinch of the incense and place it on the censer. Watching the smoke curling upwards, you lift your gaze to the statue. Whose face do you see? Which deity smiles down on you? Is it one you have met before? If they are unknown to you, what or who do they remind you of? If you were to know their name, what would it be?

Could you try to have a dialogue with them now? Is there something you would like them to help you with? Perhaps you need guidance on how to manage a range of different symptoms, or how to cope with the sudden emotional changes you feel. What might they ask you to do for them in return? How long will you work with them for? Agree these terms on both sides. When you are happy that you have said all you need to say, and heard all you need to hear (or feel), then give thanks.

It is now time to leave the temple. You can come back here whenever you like – all you need to do is find a quiet spot as you have today and use your imagination.

If you struggle to visualise this scene, use whichever sensory system works for your body – you can feel your way to the temple, or do it with sound if that feels right. When you are ready to return to everyday wakefulness, place your awareness back on your breathing and take three deep breaths, becoming increasingly wakeful with each one.

When you are back in the present, consider how, in your waking life, you might honour the particular deity you met. Perhaps you might create an altar for that divine feminine crone or warrior deity, or dedicate an area of your life to them. For example, when I was beginning my journey with my own patron deity, with whom I have worked for about five years now, I originally committed to one calendar month with a particular task of managing my energy levels. They and I agreed that in that month, I would fulfil one act of devotion each day – a prayer read out to the sky, an incense made, a chant sung to the water as I swam or walked, a yoga session done in their honour. At the end of the month, we were so bonded that I agreed to continue for another year, and I haven't looked back. My home now has a shrine to this deity in every room.

DISEMBARKING: AUTUMNAL EQUINOX AND FINDING BALANCE IN (PERI)MENOPAUSE

Elizabeth also learned that strength came in numbers. When one woman struggled with what she might become when her daughter finally left home to go into the world and form a new family, the women gathered round. They encouraged her, and held the space for her fear, holding aloft the light of inspiration so that she might see the path through the woods and not stumble. The path would lead to being a grandmother and, while it marked a change, it was not an ending – merely the beginning of a new way of being.

Elizabeth knew this change would be coming for her too, perhaps sooner than she thought, and she would have to be ready. But she also knew that, through the experiences of her circle, she was growing, and learning, and preparing herself. She was preparing to find balance by sharing in the experiences of others.

While it can be tempting to close ourselves off and retreat into the nunnery at this point in our lives, the way aristocratic women sometimes did in the past, we must just pick ourselves up and keep moving forwards. But that can make us feel as if we are just existing, so how do we reconnect to our joy, so that we can start enjoying life again?

Whether you have nurtured children or a career, you can start to feel deeply depleted and down on your resources at this time. It is likely that this is due, in part, to the imbalance of your hormones, as well as other resources in your body, such as nutrients and energy. Perhaps this is time to think about where you might have been allowing yourself to run continually on empty, and pause for a moment on the path through the menopausal woods. We can do this by (again) taking inspiration from the natural world around us.

The autumn equinox, around 22 September, is the night when we acknowledge that – just for a moment – we are poised in a state of balance between darkness and light, before the earth turns into the dark half of the year and we begin the process of wintering. This is the time for us to get out the slow cooker and start nourishing our bodies with food that was born deep within the belly of the earth – those lovely root vegetable and legume stews and soups that can be so healthy for a body that is struggling to regulate energy levels. There is also something deeply healing about allowing yourself the time to retreat into your blanket fort, if that's what you need, with a tall pile of books to read and a sense of peacefulness to counteract the daily struggles of family and working lives. But perhaps also it might be time to start looking into the various medical treatments that might help you to restore a bit of balance. My feeling is that if you combine all of these approaches into a gentle-though-intensive programme of self-care, you may start to recover your sense of equilibrium, and bring yourself back to life. For autumn – though winding down – is full of life still: red admirals are on the wing; ivy bees are searching out pollen; the hedgerows are full of seed heads, hips and haws.

This time is also an invitation to look at your inner landscape and to think about what you want to take into the next stage of your life. What do you want to hang on to? What do you want to let go? And what do you want to begin anew?

TRY THIS: A RITUAL TO CELEBRATE YOUR BODY AND MENOPAUSE

Too many of us spend too much of our lives berating our bodies or resenting them for not doing what we want them to do. Either we are too fat or too thin, too ill or too old, and we very rarely celebrate the miraculous vessels they are for our consciousness. How often do we celebrate the fact that they have grown of their own accord and continued to find strength and resilience no matter what has been thrown at them? This ritual is designed to give you the opportunity to thank your body for its perseverance thus far, and to release it (and you) from the need to seek perfection. Like all the rituals in this book, it can be done alone or in a group, depending on your own needs.

Start by preparing an altar space in the centre of the room. On it you can place any images or items that represent your divine helper, whichever deity you decided to work with in the last exercise. If you are working with a group of friends, you can each place a representation of your own favourite deities here. Also, place on the altar items that represent your body – a photograph or a drawn picture or an item it needs to 'stay afloat'. For example, if you are asthmatic, you might place your inhaler there. If there is other medication you need, place that on the altar too – whatever speaks to you of the complex relationship we can all have with our bodies. Decorate the spaces around the items on your altar with candles and flowers.

You will need:

* A pen and paper for each person
* A censer with some incense (you could use the home incense from page 23, referring back to the instructions there on how to burn incense safely. Alternatively, use an incense stick and holder of your choice)
* A red or orange candle
* A dish of water
* A dish of earth or salt
* Some favourite food and drink to share

Before you begin the ritual, figure out where the points of the compass are situated, so that you know what to do when I ask you to turn towards the east. Now I would like you (and your companions) to spend some time with a pen and paper considering what you think of as your body's worst failing. Is it an illness you carry? Is it the way (peri)menopause is making you feel? Is it the allergies that have accompanied you through life? Perhaps it's your decreasing fertility? Write a list of those 'failings'.

Next, I want you to reframe those things. What have you gained from them? This is no way to diminish any suffering or pain, but perhaps the 'failings' you listed have taught you to slow down? To appreciate the incredible strength that your body *does* have? Perhaps you have had to learn to accept the help of others or to do things differently as a consequence?

If you were to write a letter to your younger self, giving them advice about how to approach the challenges ahead, what would you tell them? Go ahead and write that letter now.

When you are all ready, dress in whatever makes you feel most confident and comfortable. I prefer to have clothes that are set aside for ritual as then they feel special when I put them on, which helps me to build a ritual mood at the right time. Perhaps it's a robe you wear just for ritual, or even a tutu and a tiara. Whatever works for you. Light the candles and incense in the space you are working in. Put on some relaxing music in the background if the mood takes you. Gather around the altar, and each take a turn in saying the following lines (or say all of them yourself if you are working alone):

> Person One: We, of this circle, gather here beneath
> the stars, on the body of this earth, to give thanks
> for our bodies, and to honour them.

Person Two: The bodies that have carried us from birth, and will carry us until death, and then back again.

Person Three: The bodies we have used and abused, that have, uncomplainingly, accepted what we have given them.

All turn and face the east, as Person One places some incense on the censer and says:

With the breath of my body, I lift my voice to the air and sing in thanks for my body. Thanks to the air for the thoughts that I give voice to.

All turn and face the south as Person Two lights the orange or red candle and says:

With the spirit of my body, I raise my energy to the fire to sing in thanks for the healing and the warmth it brings to my body.

All turn and face the west, as Person Three lifts the dish of water and says:

I give thanks to the waters for the blood of my body, which flowed in my youth, my adulthood. While it may cease to flow in this life, I give thanks to the waters for the emotions that wash through me, cleansing my soul and strengthening my love.

All turn and face the north, as Person Four lifts the dish of earth and says:

> With my body and my presence here, I give thanks
> to my body and the earth that nourishes it, that
> gives me a home, that nurtures and mothers me.

Spread out around the room, filling the space with your breath and your energy. Each of you can then go to the central altar one by one, bringing with you your letters to your younger selves. If you are feeling safe and brave enough to do so, take it in turns to read them aloud to the room. Otherwise, it is fine to each take a little time at the altar in silent dialogue with your patron god and your body.

When you have read the letter (either to yourself or the room), pass the paper over each of the four elements – beginning with the incense smoke for air, the candle flame for fire, the water dish for water, and the bowl of earth. You have now consecrated your letter in the elements, and words spoken aloud hold power.

Each person now says the following in turn:

> I offer thanks to the earth for my body, for its sus-
> tenance, its healing and its strength. I give thanks
> for my circle: may we sustain each other when
> life gets tough. May we carry each other when we
> become tired. May we feed one another when
> we become hungry.

This is the moment at which you might like to share the food and drink.

When you are ready to end the ritual, turn to the east as Person One says:

> We give thanks to the air for our breath.

Turn to the south as Person Two says:

> We give thanks to the fire for our courage.

Turn to the west as Person Three says:

> We give thanks to the water for keeping us flowing through life.

Turn to the north as Person Four says:

> We give thanks to the earth for our bodies.

Turn to the central altar again, all facing each other, and say together:

> Our sacred circle may scatter to the four winds, but we will always return to the centre. With love, happiness and the life and bodies that bond us.

At this time, you can choose what you want to do with your letters – and each person may decide on something different, because you are learning to speak your own truths aloud. You might decide to burn your letter (if you can do so safely) or bury it in the earth or simply tuck it inside your journal, to look back on it later.

Hopefully the exercises in this chapter will have guided you towards a more balanced path through your autumnal woods, taking you to a place where you start to feel more like yourself again. This is the trail we will continue to explore, as we step forward into self-actualisation.

CHAPTER EIGHT

THE JOURNEY TOWARDS REACHING YOUR POTENTIAL – SELF-ACTUALISATION

You were born with wings.
You are not meant for crawling, so don't.
You have wings.
Learn to use them and fly.

Rūmi

TAROT CARD: The World

I was once on a training course where there were a number of high-achieving young men. One day during coffee break, I came back to find them all huddled together, whispering in low tones, but displaying signs of excitement and awe. I'll admit that my curiosity was piqued and, while they were high achievers, they also assumed I was too (spot the imposter feelings in play). I asked them what I was missing out on.

'Carl's wife has decided to go all out for enlightenment in this lifetime,' one of them told me. To be honest, I wasn't sure what to reply to that, so I fudged a response that sounded suitably impressed and then moved along. I am not sure, even now, that I would know what to say.

To my mind, 'enlightenment' and 'self-actualisation' are quite similar concepts. If you hang around long enough with people studying self- or spiritual development, you are likely to hear one or both terms being used interchangeably to imply that someone has reached the zenith of their spiritual journey. But what does that actually mean, and what exactly do I mean by self-actualisation?

Self-actualisation can generally be thought of as the full realisation of one's creative, intellectual and social potential through internal drivers (versus external rewards such as money, status or power). The term comes to us from the field of psychology, and commonly brings in the work of two different psychologists, Abraham Maslow (1908–70) and Carl Rogers (1902–87).

This chapter, like that coffee-break conversation on the training course, is probably the most abstract in the book. Yet having navigated all those winding paths through the woods, it's really important for us to think about what these significant life experiences might add up to and where we take ourselves next. We want to be able to move forward in a 'good orderly direction', as the writer Julia Cameron puts it in her book on the spiritual path to creativity, *The Artist's Way*.

So, I would invite you to pause with me in this particular glade of the woods, and look at how autumn is visible around you. If you are starting to live your life in a way that is influenced by those internal drivers, rather than the external ones, you might be noticing that the forests and the gardens are now filled with another kind of abundance. While we might not always have monetary abundance where we would like it, the apple trees in my friend's garden hang heavy with apples in the autumn, and in the wood we start to see all manner of mushrooms growing – making me pause over their variety and their names. Whoever took on the task of naming all the fungus must have taken a delight in doing so – I discover dryad's saddle mounting an oak trunk, its colouring reminiscent of the feathers of the pheasants that create such a racket by bursting out of the undergrowth in a riot of feathers and squawking. Deeper in, chicken of the woods alights on a beech stump – tantalisingly close, yet too far up to reach. Then this year – a treat. I discover fly agaric mushrooms – their red and white fairy-tale colours brilliant in the morning sunshine – as they nestle beneath a birch tree.

So as we take in the beauty of what is around us in the natural world, perhaps we might begin to explore what self-actualisation is through the psychological lens, as that will give us a sense of how we might move towards it. How do we reach that elusive plateau where we can remain strong to changes and challenges, like a tree facing an autumn storm? If self-actualisation means reaching that place, can we finally say we understand our reason for being? (And, if not, how can we achieve this?) Can we finally present ourselves, unapologetically, to the world, without feeling the need to justify our very bodies and our existence? Let's find out. As with other chapters, there are some exercises for you to explore with your journal, and a ritual at the end to help you step into your own shaft of sunlight when it comes piercing through the trees.

READING THE MAP: WHAT IS SELF-ACTUALISATION?

Elizabeth and her friends had fallen into the habit of meeting once a month, when the moon shone full, and they would focus on whatever was current in their lives. Sometimes they gave thanks for the reaping of the harvest in autumn, at others they talked about their cares for the winter that would inevitably come round again. Elizabeth found, as they marked the passing of time and the seasons, that she almost wondered if those seasons would stop if their congregations came to an end.

As an undergraduate, there was one area of study I always found endlessly fascinating, even after the usual late nights, and that was behavioural psychology. Specifically, I have come back time and again to the work of Abraham Maslow. Maslow was an American psychologist engaged in how we reach our full potential as human beings. As part of his work, he produced a model known as 'Maslow's Hierarchy of Needs' to explain how we can each reach a place of 'self-actualisation' where we are able to do our best work, achieve all that we set out to do and feel happy and fulfilled. This might sound like some form of nirvana, but Maslow was more concerned with this life, right now, than with some future paradise.

According to Maslow, the key to success is to get the foundations right before you try to move up a layer in what he saw as a pyramid (see illustration opposite). For example, he believed that you can't self-actualise if you are worrying about basic physical needs such as warmth and shelter or if you are lonely, have issues with self-esteem or little sense of belonging. Likewise, if you are coping with bereavement, the end of a significant relationship or worries about money or employment, in this model those elements have to be secured before you can move up to the next level.

I can sense that you might be thinking, 'Right, I might as well give up now', given all the elements that self-actualisation seems to require. Or maybe you're looking at this and considering all the people it excludes. For example, is it suggesting that people with long-term health conditions can never reach a point of self-actualisation? If our model of the world is a pyramid shape, it implies that we have to keep climbing ever upward, where we might never reach the top. Also, to my mind, the idea of a mountain is not quite the same as an exploration of the woodland, where we pause in childlike wonder over our discoveries and see the magic that's around us. If life is a mountain and not a wood, then surely the emphasis is on the climb and not the immersion?

Unsurprisingly, Maslow received criticism for some aspects of his theory, and alternative studies have given mixed results. But before we give up all hope, it's important to remember that this is just a model. Later in his career, Maslow himself wrote that the hierarchy is not necessarily a fixed order. Very like Kübler-Ross's stages of grief (see Chapter One), life has many more twists and turns than a model can ever show. So, while we are navigating each part of the woods, each significant life event, we might move between the different stages of grief or the different layers of Maslow's hierarchy. It's important to remember that, as I have said before, the map is not the territory; it is only meant as a guide. It doesn't do to have your eyes glued to the map while missing the landscape of your life – and of possibility – right in front of you.

What I think is really useful about Maslow's model, however, is the visual reminder it gives us to hold back on beating ourselves up when we are struggling with massive life changes. If your relationship has just ended or you are worried about a family member or grieving in any way, don't be surprised if you are struggling to achieve that lofty ambition you have in mind for yourself. How could you? It would be hugely tough – impossible, even – to be 'living your best life' under those circumstances. Some situations are just terrible, and we can sit with our emotions at those times, pulling in all the support we need, and give ourselves the space to feel and to heal.

TRY THIS: PREPARING FOR THE JOURNEY: JOURNALING TOWARDS SELF-ACTUALISATION

Self-reflection is one of the crucial skills of an actualised person, and journaling can really help navigate this. Using your notebook and pen, spend some time (undisturbed if you can) free-writing a response to the following questions:

- Where in your life do you feel a sense of fulfilment?
- When was the last time you felt genuinely content and in a state of 'flow'? Where were you, and what were you doing?
- How might you increase this in your life or make more time for those activities? For example, if gardening, yoga or volunteering gives you the greatest satisfaction, could you choose to wake up an hour earlier to do that thing before anything else? Or perhaps your working hours could be rearranged to allow you more dedicated time? Don't cut off any options with a 'but that wouldn't work because . . .'
- How can you give back to others? Is there any other overlap between the things that give you fulfilment, your community and that sense of 'flow'?

- What was the last new idea you took on board? Where were you and what was the idea?
- How do your current relationships nurture you? How do you nurture your loved ones in return?
- How often do you take time like this for self-reflection and contemplation? How might you create more of these opportunities in your life?
- How do you bring new ideas, thoughts and knowledge into your life?

These are all questions that psychologists have suggested indicate that we are on the road to self-actualisation – when we begin to consider and explore them in earnest. But don't worry if you are not there yet – this is something to be developed over time, should you wish. If there are areas that you don't currently feel comfortable with, perhaps there is a way to gently bring them to your awareness, so that you can steer your course in that direction. As you go, remember to stay curious and supportive of your own development.

STEERING YOUR COURSE: THE TOP OF MASLOW'S PYRAMID

There was one woman in particular for whom Elizabeth was full of admiration. Beira was a little older than Elizabeth, but had the quiet confidence and wisdom that came from long life. Beira was quick to laugh, and kind, and when any of the women stumbled and fell in their lives, it was often Beira who gathered them up and gave them a warm embrace. Beira lived alone and peacefully in the woods, and she reminded Elizabeth a little of Margaret. Beira travelled everywhere with a basket of special things and, whatever the need was, she seemed to have the

right gift in her basket. Just being with her made Elizabeth feel calm,
nourished and blessed.

So now that we've considered those layers in Maslow's model, let's have a look at the top of the pyramid and the qualities he suggests we might hold in mind when it comes to aiming for self-actualisation ourselves. Our last 'Try This' was pointing us in this direction.

Maslow looked at public figures such as Eleanor Roosevelt and Albert Einstein for clues and suggested that actuated people had several qualities in common. They tended to accept their flaws, as well as those of other people, usually with humour. They were resourceful, independent, able to form their own opinions autonomously and didn't require external powers to intervene in their lives for a sense of validation or progression. They were able to form deep, loving relationships with others and were adept at discerning between truth and lies, while also exuding a sense of gratitude. Lastly, they saw their lives as having a deeper purpose beyond their needs alone. Yet while Maslow created the model by looking at prominent figures, he also applied his theory to ordinary, everyday people, explaining that:

> A musician must make music, an artist must paint, a poet must write, if he is to be ultimately at peace with himself. What a man can be, he must be. This need we call self-actualisation . . . It refers to the desire for self-fulfilment, namely, to the tendency for him to become actualised in what he is potentially . . . to become everything that one is capable of becoming.

What Maslow is telling us is that self-actualisation is about reaching your fullest potential, but especially in those areas of life that you are passionate about. It's not about power, money or reputation, but about identifying those pleasures and making sure you do more of them in a way that is entirely true to those desires.

Carl Rogers, another psychologist working in this field around the same time as Maslow, re-termed actualisation as 'the fully functioning person'. One benefit of Rogers' expansion of Maslow's theory is that self-actualisation becomes an ongoing journey in itself rather than a destination we climb towards. He also defined five essential characteristics. According to Rogers, the fully functioning person:

- Is open to all experiences (both positive and negative)
- Can live fully in the present and only in the moment, which Rogers described as 'existential living'
- Can trust their feelings and act on them accordingly
- Is creative, both in their thinking and in their ability to adapt and change to circumstances
- Seeks out new experiences, and through doing so has a sense of being fulfilled

What Maslow and Rogers were describing is reaching a place where how we act and present ourselves to the outside world, unapologetically and with passion, matches how we see ourselves. I think that's something we can all get on board with as we look to the future.

TRY THIS: REWRITING YOUR OWN STORY

For this 'Try This' I would like you to combine two of the tools you have been using throughout the book – your diary (in whatever form you are using it) and your tarot deck. Think back over some of the stories of your life, particularly the ones that have come up for you during the reading of this book – those big life changes we have been exploring. Consider the narrative you give each one – your version of why things happened and why those changes took place. Decide which one you would like to hone in on.

Thinking about that one big change, start to shuffle your tarot cards. When the time feels right, pick out three cards and place them face up in front of you. They represent past, present and future.

Have a look at the cards. Do they tell a narrative that differs wildly from your own?

- If so, how is it different?
- Start to focus in on the feeling it gives you. Is it positive or does it feel uncomfortable?
- Is there a 'truth' you can take away from the cards that may show a slightly different perspective on the narrative you have always told yourself about this life change? Do you gain something in the retelling of this story?
- If it jars for you, can you approach the story with a sense of childlike curiosity instead of revulsion (or whatever response it elicits)?

Both Maslow and Rogers talk of self-actuating people as being open to new experiences, both positive and negative, with no prejudice about accepting new information. If we can start to explore some of our own experiences and see them not only as the source of severe trauma, but also as the great teachers they often are, we can begin to live in a way that allows past hurts to become less triggering and approach new experiences with that same sense of being open-hearted.

SETTING OUT: WASHING AWAY THE PAST

One day Elizabeth was walking through the woods with Beira on the way to their swimming spot. The women had taken to dipping in the river before their gatherings, and on the way Beira started to point out to Elizabeth all the wonders they could see in the forest. First it was a cluster of tiny, red-tipped mushrooms, almost imperceptible to the naked eye. Then a cache of hazelnuts set aside by a squirrel to see it through the winter. Each item they saw made Elizabeth catch her breath.

Sometimes it can feel as if we never reach a level of self-actualisation, but instead catch brief moments of something akin to it. Just when you think you have reached a particular conclusion about life, a new experience presents itself and you must re-assess what you thought you knew. This means those fleeting moments of peace are precious when they come. When I was going through my last big period of transformation and reassessment, I found immersion in cold water particularly therapeutic. It's no surprise that when we realise our own bodies are made up of 70 per cent water, the tides found in nature also show up in the human body. Water connects us with nature. In many religions, immersion in water is seen as an energetic and spiritual cleansing, as well as a physical one. Our Jewish cousins employ the use of a *mikvah*, or ritual bath. Some Christian sects use immersion in water as part of a baptismal rite of passage, while in the Hindu faith bathing in the sacred river Ganges in India on certain occasions is reputed to bring forgiveness for transgressions.

For me, wild swimming has provided some rich and deep encounters with nature, but it also brings that sense of an energetic cleansing. I have several favourite swimming spots, and swim weekly with a group of women. In those special places, I have watched the seasons turn, swum among golden autumn leaves and seen a king-fisher bobbing on a branch as I swam below her. I have also observed the life cycle of the dragonfly play out, watched adult dragonflies flying fast across the surface of the water – electric blues and greens, mingling with iridescent black and reds. I have seen those adult dragonflies emerging from the outer casing of their nymph bodies on the side of a pool, and seen the translucent shell-bodies remaining, left attached to a tree root at the edge of the water. In most parts of the world, dragonflies symbolise speed and agility – they are able to fly with speed and can change direction in a full 360-degree turning circle, due to their unique wing positioning. In Swedish culture they indicate the purity of a person's soul, while among the Navajo people of the United States they symbolise purity and happiness. Dragonflies remind us to be flexible and adaptable to new growth; they tell us that new beginnings are always on their way.

TRY THIS: IMMERSION IN WATER TO WASH AWAY THE PAST AND FIND YOUR EQUILIBRIUM

If you're intending to immerse yourself in wild water, make sure you don't stay in for very long unless you have a regular practice and the means to warm up again afterwards. Starting wild swimming is not advised in the middle of winter as the temperature drops can be too sudden. Pack warm, dry clothing, a warm drink, and go with a friend. Don't swim anywhere unless you know it is safe to do so – pollution levels and currents can make seemingly beautiful spots hazardous if you don't know them – if you're unsure, look at the wild swimming website for further advice, and do check interactive sea or river pollution maps online in advance (the links for these websites are in the chapter notes at the back of the book). It's best to avoid wild swimming entirely if there has been recent heavy rainfall or a storm, as sewage and farming waste are likely to have been washed into the river and the water may be in spate. In winter, why not visit a heated outdoor pool in your area, or think about moving the ritual indoors?

To do this exercise, go to your chosen natural body of water, be it the sea, river or lake, or your own bathroom at home (remember – water is still natural even if it comes out of a tap). If you are doing this in your bathtub, throw in a handful of sea salt, a natural energy cleanser. Sit for a while by the water and think about the experience you've been going through. How is it changing you? How are you transforming like the dragonfly? Who are the people who have shown up for you, who have surprised you? It's often in times of adversity that we discover who our real support network is. I would invite you to close your eyes if you can, and take three deep breaths, focusing on the sensation of air filling your lungs.

Notice how your body is feeling – are there any aching points, any twinges, any parts that are giving you discomfort? Notice them and be kind to yourself in your thoughts. This body carries you through life and is, for the moment, the vessel in which you exist. Unlike the dragonfly, you don't get to leave it behind just yet.

Now it is time to prepare to go into the water. Dip in your toes to begin with, and get in gradually, especially in a natural body of water. Immerse your feet. Feel the silky sensation of the water as it touches your skin. Is it cold? Is it warm? Next, step in up to your calves and up to your knees. Feel the current of the water. Is it still or moving more quickly? Does it come in waves or does it flow? Immerse up to your stomach and waist. Focus on the water's embrace, how your legs feel supported. Then up to your chest. If you're in a bath, consider its warmth. If you're in a natural body of water, think about its coolness.

Now allow yourself to immerse your arms, feeling the water gently clasping your hands, as you return its embrace. Does it feel silken on your neck, or is its coldness sharp?

Take another deep breath and focus again on the life change you're experiencing – the sheer length and breadth of the changes you're undergoing. You've come this far and you've made so much progress. Give yourself a mental pat on the back for the bravery you've shown.

Another deep breath and it's time to immerse. If you're able to allow yourself full immersion, then I'd invite you to do so; if not, just wet the top of your head with some of the water on your hands. I'm not always comfortable with full immersion, and I find this version just as effective.

As the water touches your face and the top of your head, imagine that it's washing away the old you, carrying it downstream, or out to sea, or down the plughole. You are washing away the layers of your old self, just like a dragonfly emerging from its adolescent body into its full-grown, adult, colourful being. We are now allowing the new you to emerge fully, in all its beautiful strength.

When you feel ready, get out, dry off and warm up: welcome your rejuvenated self to the world.

I often find cold water immersion can change the way I see everything – colours can seem brighter, and I am ready to go back into nature and open my eyes to the wonder of what is around me.

FINDING YOUR SENSE OF CHILDLIKE WONDER AND JOY; FINDING COMFORT IN CHANGE

Elizabeth seized the opportunity to ask Beira about herself, imagining that in order to be so at peace, Beira must have had a quiet and happy life, one that was filled with many loving experiences and years of ease. She said as much to Beira, who turned to Elizabeth and laughed, her eyes alight with amusement and kindness.

Several years ago, I met up with an old school friend who has had very different life experiences from me on her adult journey through the woods. Some really tough life events that she has had to assimilate and deal with. The life that she dreamed of creating when we used to test out our slightly rebellious adult wings together when we were eighteen could have cut her off at the roots completely, but it didn't. Instead, she rose above those experiences and chose to keep moving forwards with a sense of childlike awe.

When we got together recently we were exploring a region of France that she knew well, but that I had never visited before. We shopped for new clothes together, visited a spa where they had a 'rainforest experience' that played sound and lights while you showered, and went out gathering fresh walnuts in the fields around her house. We ate new foods, explored villages and churches around the area, and swam in the unheated pool at her home. She laughed about me being the perfect travelling companion, because everything she showed me elicited one response: 'That's amazing!' Rather than seeing this as a sign of naivety, it became our mantra for the week.

One day as we sat in a café overlooking a woodland area, we talked about the fact that we believed, quite firmly, that adult life was a series of experiences that you had to live through, but that when you reach the tail end of them you realise that you had the right approach to life when you were a teenager. In spite of all the knowledge that our 'adult selves' have accrued, in many ways our young adult identities were the ones that understood better what the world is about: wonder.

Another friend, Francesco Dimitri, has written a book on how to capture those miracles of everyday life. Francesco writes that it is this sense of wonder that drives every scientific or artistic endeavour, as well as every spiritual enquiry we make. That feeling of our curiosity being fired up by what is in front of us is one of the most fruitful drivers in human existence. The point, Francesco says, is not to revert to some strange hybrid child-adult, but to feel happier and more fulfilled in our adult lives, where we are better equipped to face the challenges that meet us at every turn of the woodland path because we have our eyes open and our bodies alive to the possibilities.

It is this sense of awe that gives us the flexibility to bend and adapt to life's changes and approach each day with a hopeful curiosity, instead of holding a rigid mould that everything has to fit into. If, like me, you spend time in nature, you will be accustomed to watching the minute changes that happen, day by day, witnessing each one with a sense of anticipation and excitement. Having a daily practice of getting outside means that I see the small details of nature as each season turns. My first hope with this book is to have introduced you to some of those practices that help develop a meaningful and fulfilling relationship with this beautiful planet we call home, which can only be a good thing in the face of mounting ecological concern. It is very difficult to disrespect something you have a loving relationship with. My second hope is that by observing nature you can be reassured that change is absolutely normal for all of us.

As I wrote in my grief memoir:

Strange how we always assume that the truth is a rigid thing that always remains fixed. So much of society is built around 'the truth' that is fixed and never changing, like a granite dolmen that stands tall against an ever-changing sky. The 'truth' is that even granite changes over time. Its face is weathered by the driving rain, the howling wind and the warm summer sun. We are all constantly in a state of flux, and the only thing that never changes is that one thing: that the world, and we in it, are ever changing.

TRY THIS: REACHING TOWARDS YOUR OWN SELF-ACTUALISATION

Although in Wicca we talk about the changing seasons as the Wheel of the Year, I actually think of the wheel as a spiral, not a flat circle. Each year as the seasons pass, we learn to go a little deeper into each sabbat or festival, and I always learn something new from the people who join me in my classes, or the circles or events I attend. We all keep learning, growing and adapting as life continues to revolve.

To manage your expectations, this exercise is not going to give you a final definitive answer on the existential 'Why are we here?' question. That's not how it works. Instead, we are going to be making use of a tool I learned in coaching, adapting it to suit our purposes.

If I were ever to draw you a map of the woods of life, I think it might look like this circle, which – like the wheel – you can consider as a spiral to be returned to over and over again. Each woodland grove that we enter gives us a new experience, and a new learning that must then be integrated into our personality and our values, before we move on to explore the next spinney. What I mean by 'integrated' is that in working these areas through, in spending time considering and feeling their effects, you reach a point where they don't feel like a burning dustbin each time you think about them. For example, grieving for my mother still has the capacity to floor me from time to time, but on a day-to-day basis I can function well, I can remember the good times we shared and I can even talk about her quite comfortably with others.

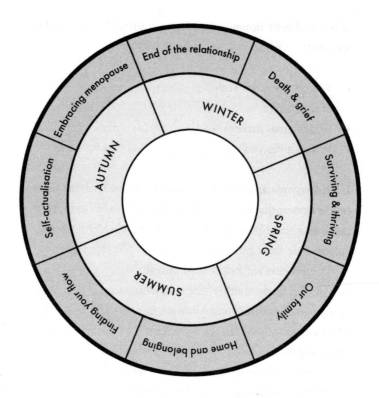

So, how do we do this thing?

If you want to do this alone, some quiet, uninterrupted time with your journal is ideal. However, it also works well with a friend and a glass of your favourite tipple (soft or otherwise).

Sit down with your copy of this map and think about how it applies to your own life. Don't expect your own wheel to look exactly like mine. If there are areas you want to add, go ahead and include them. For example, if you have experienced a significant life change that isn't covered in these pages, pencil it in under whichever season you feel suits it best. Looking at your adapted wheel, think about and note down (in whatever journal format works for you):

- Which areas of your life contribute to your feeling of wellbeing
- Which areas make you feel uncertain or unhappy
- Which areas you want to change or to integrate further

If it helps, you can number the areas from one to three, with one indicating that you are not yet where you want to be, two being an average 'meh' and three being fabulous. You can even colour-code those numbers if you like.

This process will help you to identify areas that you wish to work on further, either alone or with friends, a support group or a therapist. You might want to go back and spend a little more time in the chapter that relates to that theme or season, using the suggested activities to explore the topic further.

It is important to remember that no one doing this exercise would have a completely sorted map of their woods – we are living, breathing souls who are always going through a process. Its rare for me to reach a plateau in my woodland explorations, and the map will be constantly changing, just as life does.

ARRIVING AND DISEMBARKING: SELF-ACTUALISATION

'Oh, dear one,' said Beira, 'is that what you think?' She shook her head and took a deep breath. 'Life for me has not been a rose garden filled with sweet-scented blossoms,' she continued. 'It's been hard work every step of the way. Some years I have wondered what on earth the gods can throw at me next. But you know,' Beira pondered aloud, 'someone wise once told me that you had to be prepared to suffer to learn, and that our gods

enter into this relationship with us openly. They give us a choice. We can choose the quiet primrose path to a steady life where not much happens, or we can choose the path to wisdom and learning. That path is rocky sometimes, and you may stumble and land face down in the mud. But it is also filled with wonder, and awe, and experiences that will change us for the better. The gods never give us more than we can manage. Which do you think I chose now?' asked Beira, smiling broadly.

This section is going to be the shortest one in the book, because the simple truth is that our journey towards self-actualisation or enlightenment is an ongoing process – it isn't a destination at all. Surprise! For this journey through the woods, the best advice I can give you is this: look around and witness the miracle of the life you continue to create. It's a beautiful thing, in all its imperfections.

TRY THIS: A RITUAL TO COMMIT TO YOUR OWN SELF-ACTUALISATION

While most of the rituals in this book have been created in the spirit of marking a rite of passage, this one acknowledges self-actualisation as a continuous process. As my beloved Mr Tolkien put it, roads go ever ever on. If we continue our lives with a sense of open curiosity, rather than needing to seek perfection or completion in all things, then we will, I believe, attain self-actualisation. This ritual, then, is to mark your commitment to that process. As with all the rituals in this book, it can be done alone or in a group.

You will need:

* A pine cone for each participant – in autumn you may find these in abundance in your local pine wood
* A dish of your favourite seasonal berries, all mixed up

* Some slips of paper and a pen for each participant
* A white candle to place on the central altar
* A royal blue or purple candle for each participant, in a candle holder you can move without dripping wax on yourself
* A glass of red wine, grape juice or blackcurrant juice for each participant
* An altar space in the centre of the room with a blue or purple cloth. On it you can place any images or items that represent your passions and great enjoyments in life. Decorate the spaces around the items on your altar with candles and flowers.

Prepare the space by cleaning and cleansing it with incense or salt and water. Light the altar's white candle, and face to the east.

If doing this alone, you can say each of the following lines yourself. If doing it with friends, allocate a 'guardian' role to each person and divide the lines up among you.

Eastern Guardian:

> We call upon the guardians of the eastern quarter
> to guard and witness our rite. With the power of
> air and words, inspire us to our best endeavours.

All turn to face the south.

Southern Guardian:

> We call upon the guardians of the south to
> guard and witness our rite. With the power of
> fire and passion, give us the courage to fulfil our
> best endeavours.

All turn to face the west.
  Western Guardian:

> We call upon the guardians of the west to guard
> and witness our rite. With the power of water
> and compassion, give us the emotional purity to
> support our best endeavours.

All turn to face the north.
  Northern Guardian:

> We call upon the guardians of the north to guard
> and witness our rite. With the power of earth
> and strength, give us the stability to support our
> best endeavours.

All turn to face the centre and each other (If you are doing
this alone, face the central altar.)
  Eastern Guardian:

> I came upon a woodland clearing at dawn, and
> heard the sound of the breeze in the falling beech
> leaves. They whispered to me of my purpose in
> life, and reminded me I could always seek solace
> beneath their branches.

The eastern guardian lights their blue or purple candle, using
the central candle as the source.
  Southern Guardian:

> I came upon the woods at noon, underneath the
> sovereign sun, and the oak tree spoke of my place

in this world, and my value as part of it. Me, the sun and the oak – all in perfect synergy.

The southern guardian lights their blue or purple candle.
Western Guardian:

I wandered down a woodland path at dusk, just as the sky was dimming and the robin was singing her last song of the day. The willow tree reminded me to remain flexible and bend with life, and to go with the flow of the river.

The western guardian lights their blue or purple candle.
Northern Guardian:

I stood in the centre of the woods at midnight, under a moonlit sky. The stars leaned down to whisper, and the pine tree shrugged. Of course, he told me, you will always remember your purpose, if you let me show you the way.

The northern guardian lights their blue or purple candle.

Move towards the altar and take up a pen and the slips of paper. Begin to write a single word on each, one that speaks to you of you as your best self – perhaps it will be a trigger word that reminds you to nurture yourself, or to always be your best supporter, or perhaps it will be a word from your life's purpose exercise.

Next, fold up the slips of paper until they are really small, one at a time, remembering the word inside them as you do so. As you finish folding each one, tuck it underneath the scales of your pine cone, then tip the blue or purple candle over it to seal the paper in with some drops of wax. Say each word aloud as you seal it in. Continue this process until you are all done – there is no rush.

Eastern Guardian:

> I call upon the last star at dawn and the people of my heart to witness this moment – wherever we may drift upon the earth, may the beech remind us always of this promise to ourselves.

Southern Guardian:

> I call upon the fires in our hearts and the spirit of the oak to remind us that whenever the world feels too much, we can always find courage in our hearts to stand firm and remember this promise to ourselves.

Western Guardian:

> I call upon the waters of the earth, of this beautiful blue planet, and the green of the willow tree as it trails its fingers in the water, to remind us to flow with the tides and remember our promises to ourselves.

Northern Guardian:

> I call upon the spirit of the earth and the pine to witness our promises to ourselves. I call upon the earth as it holds the pine steady, may it remind us to be rooted to ourselves. Whenever the wind

blows at our limbs and tries to uproot us, we can
always find ourselves deep within the woods, amid
the trees and the birds and the animals.

Come together, hold your pine cones up to the room and
blow on them as you say:

As we do will it, so mote it be.

Keep your pine cone somewhere safe and, whenever you feel
yourself wavering, sit for a moment, hold it against your heart
and breathe deeply as you remember the words on the paper,
tucked safely within the cone alongside the seeds of new life.

THE MANIFESTO OF THE
PERFECTLY IMPERFECT LIFE

Yet, if you enter the woods
Of a summer evening late,
When the night-air cools on the trout-ringed pools
Where the otter whistles his mate . . .
You will hear the beat of a horse's feet,
And the swish of a skirt in the dew . . .
As though they perfectly knew
The old lost road through the woods.

Rudyard Kipling

Alua Arthur, who describes herself as a Death Doula and recovering attorney, gives a fabulous TED talk called 'Why Thinking about Death Gives You a Better Life'. In it she encourages us to forget about the small details (eat the cake; let the traffic merge) and to instead consider the bigger picture. 'Leaving a legacy isn't optional,' she says:

> We're doing it every single day. You're doing it with every smile, every word, every kind word, every harsh word, every action, every inaction, every dollar that you spend.

But while you might think that would make a person paranoid about what they were leaving behind, Alua also encourages us to remember that we are beautifully, magically human, with all the messiness that includes – imperfection does not need to be seen as a negative thing.

Alua's thoughts on life chime with my own. I see us as being perfectly imperfect – no longer striving for unachievable perfection, and instead allowing our sense of childlike curiosity and wonder to take over.

I thought about how I should end this book, and considered writing ten rules for the perfectly imperfect life or perhaps specific directions for making your way through its twists and turns – but I don't want to impose rules on you. This, then, is my manifesto – a statement of my intention and motivation, but by no means a set of strictures to live by. In fact, I would encourage you to take this and think about what you might include in your own manifesto, how you might adapt my thoughts to fit *your* outlook and beliefs.

Firstly, I believe we should live our lives and love to the fullest degree possible. If there is any purpose in this brief window we call life, then it is to experience as many adventures as we can and to love those we believe in.

If people don't get you, or don't love you, then leave them behind, whoever they are or whatever relationship they claim to have with you. If they've not treated you well or loved you as you deserve to be loved, then they have no claim on you. Be fair-minded and hear people out, but don't accept excuses for bad behaviour without evidence of change.

Create something positive every day. Give yourself the gift of time amid the chaos to immerse yourself in the thing you love the most. You deserve to be able to carve out space for yourself as much as for your loved ones and the thing from which you earn a living. Wherever you find your joy, if it is not harmful to others, do it as much as you can.

When catastrophe strikes you down, go very gently on yourself, and be kind. It may take time to bounce back from adversity, and you will not be the same person you were before the events took place, but that doesn't mean a part of that person isn't still inside you somewhere. It means that the kernel at the heart of you has broken out of the seed husk. It may feel painful now, but it is starting to sprout leaves, I promise. What the leaves will grow into, you may not know yet, but there is life there and life has a tendency to push on through hardship into something new.

Immerse yourself in nature whenever you can. Respect the plants and the birds and the animals you find there, and allow your heart to quest for the wisdom they have to share.

And while I may have begun with the words of the great proto-pagan Rudyard Kipling, and indeed have ended with them, I have to point out that on his last line just above I disagree. There *is* a road through the woods, but each person's path is uniquely their own. Other people might share advice about how they navigated their way through the thorny paths, around the great boles of the oaks and larches. You may find wisdom and truth there, for sure, but ultimately the path is your own. The best source of wisdom you can possibly hold is your own intuition; you are your very best guide.

So, I would invite you to sit beneath your favourite tree, take a deep breath of the oxygen it breathes out and remember your synergy with the natural world. The tree breathes out and you breathe in; you exhale and the tree inhales. Each of you has a unique role to play in the tapestry that makes up the wild wood. It is only by listening very carefully, to yourself and to this beautiful world that surrounds us, that you will hear the voice that leads you down the winding path and through the trees to the edge of the wood.

ACKNOWLEDGEMENTS

Writing is one of the most introverted tasks, as it can involve long periods of solitude at strange hours with only the company of the page. Yet it cannot be done without the help, encouragement and input of a number of really crucial people, without whom this book couldn't have been brought to life.

Firstly, I would like to thank three women who put me back together when I was irrevocably broken by life – Lizzie Conrad Hughes, Kath Beattie and Shirley Mitchell. I would also like to thank my partner in life, John Callow, the person who has helped me learn to love again (instead of becoming a solitary dog-lady). Each chapter has begun with a walk and some stick throwing. Kath, Lizzie and John were the three people I talked over each and every chapter with – checking my ideas, chewing over the challenges and working through the knots. Inevitably, a lot of those walks took place in the rainforest near my home, so I am grateful also to the input nature has had in this book.

As well as the home team, I also have a huge debt of gratitude to the team at Elliott and Thompson who worked so tirelessly on this book. Firstly to Amy Greaves and Sarah Rigby, who first prompted the idea over lunch on Gray's Inn Road, and my agent Michael Alcock, who is never anything except encouraging. Sarah continued to support and develop the book with me, offering that temperate balance of the freedom to be myself and to be creative while asking just the right questions at the right time to tease out the detail. Also on the team – the fabulous Pippa Crane, who beautifully handled the task of keeping me on track with my research, and

Caroline Taggart, for keeping an eye on those pesky words that can sometimes move around when you are not looking. Then there is the team who help the book to take its first steps – Amy Greaves and Claire Maxwell, who have worked tirelessly to help the rest of the world hear about it.

I also need to thank my colleagues in the voluntary-sector organisation, which has been my working home for the last twenty-four years. It is here I have learned how to 'adult', and learned all the skills I have then put into practice.

And finally, I want to acknowledge you, lovely reader – the person who only becomes visible later on, when you reach out and let me know if I have hit the mark or not. If you are lost in the woods and in need of a lantern, a cloak and a map, I hope this book helps to serve as all of those things.

NOTES

Introduction

Rudyard Kipling, 'The Way through the Woods': https://www. kiplingsociety.co.uk/poem/poems_woods.htm, accessed 5 February 2023

Angela Carter, 'The Company of Wolves' in *The Bloody Chamber and Other Stories* (Vintage Classics, 1979)

Part One: Winter in the Woods

Emily Dickinson, 'There's a certain Slant of light': https://www. poetryfoundation.org/poems/45723/theres-a-certain-slant-of-light-320, accessed 28 November 2023

You should be able to source resins such as frankincense and myrrh online or at your local herbalist store.

Chapter One: The Journey Through Death and . . .

Kahlil Gibran, *The Prophet* (Heinemann, 1926)

Elisabeth Kübler-Ross and David Kessler, *On Grief and Grieving: Finding the Meaning of Grief through the Five Stages of Loss* (Simon & Schuster, 2005)

For more about Whitehorse Hill Woman: https://www.dartmoor.gov. uk/wildlife-and-heritage/heritage/bronze-age/whitehorse-hill, accessed 5 February 2023

Chapter Two: The Journey to the End of the Affair

Edna St Vincent Millay, 'Ebb': https://www.poetryfoundation.org/ poems/44720/ebb

For more about the concept of edgelands: Paul Farley and Michael Symmons Roberts, *Edgelands: Journeys into England's True Wilderness* (Vintage, 2012)

To write a letter to your future self: https://www.futureme.org, accessed 1 March 2023

David Shephard can be found at https://performancepartnership. com/about-us/david-shephard/, accessed 1 March 2023

Part Two: Spring in the Woods

D. H. Lawrence, 'Craving for Spring': https://kalliope.org/en/text/ lawrence2001060908

Chapter Three: The Journey Through New Relationships

Rabindranath Tagore, 'Unending Love': https://allpoetry.com/ Unending-Love

Samuel Taylor-Coleridge's letter about soulmates was quoted in an article about what lies behind the myth of the soulmate: https://ifstudies.org/blog/whats-behind-the-belief-in-a-soulmate, accessed 12 March 2023

Dr Shauna H. Springer on the phenomena of love, soulmates and the crack-cocaine high you sometimes feel when you are in love: https://www.psychologytoday.com/gb/blog/the-joint-adventures-well-educated-couples/201208/falling-in-love-is-smoking-crack-cocaine, accessed 13 March 2023

Bjarne M. Holmes, 'In Search of My "One-And-Only": Romance-Related Media and Beliefs in Romantic Relationship Destiny' https://cios.org/EJCPUBLIC/017/3/01735.HTML, accessed 12 March 2023

Chapter Four: The Journey Through Surviving and Thriving in Your Family

Jalāl ad-Dīn Muhammad Rūmi, *The Essential Rumi*, translated by Coleman Barks and John Moyne (Penguin, 1995)

Gabor Maté, *In the Realm of Hungry Ghosts* (Vermilion, 2018). For more about Maté's work: https://drgabormate.com/book/ in-the-realm-of-hungry-ghosts/, accessed 8 July 2023

The quote from the *Tao Te Ching* is taken from a translation by John H. McDonald (Arcturus, 2009)

Quote from *Psychology Today*: https://www.psychologytoday.com/gb/basics/family-dynamics, accessed 3 April 2023

The statistics came from the Office of National Statistics website: https://www.ons.gov.uk/peoplepopulationandcommunity/births deathsandmarriages/families/bulletins/familiesandhouseholds/2020, accessed 3 April 2023

Peggy O'Donnell Heffington, 'Why Women Not Having Kids Became a Panic': https://www.nytimes.com/2023/05/06/opinion/women-without-children-history.html, accessed 27 September 2023

Danielle McGeough, 'Family Stories: Fragments and Identity' in *Storytelling, Self, Society*, January–April 2012, vol. 8, no. 1, pp. 17–26

Part Three: Summer in the Woods

Mary Webb, 'The Secret Joy', *The Spring of Joy* (Jonathan Cape, 1928)

Chapter Five: The Journey Towards Finding Your Flow or Your Perfect Career

The quote is from the headstone of John Keats, in the Protestant Cemetery in Rome.

The quote from Bill Bailey is mentioned here: https://www.brainyquote.com/quotes/bill_bailey_1064295, accessed 24 March 2023

Chris Cancialosi, 'It's All in Your Head: How to Achieve Mastery and Improve Performance': https://www.forbes.com/sites/chriscancialosi/2016/08/30/its-all-in-your-head-how-to-achieve-mastery-and-improve-performance/?sh=4d65c975cac5, accessed 24 March 2023. In it, Cancialosi cites Malcolm Gladwell's book, *Outliers: The Story of Success* (Penguin, 2009).

Elizabeth Gilbert, *Big Magic: Creative Living Beyond Fear* (Bloomsbury, 2015)

Doreen Valiente, *The Charge of the Goddess* (The Doreen Valiente Foundation and the Centre for Pagan Studies, 2014)

Ruchika Tulshyan and Jodi-Ann Burey, 'Stop Telling Women They Have Imposter Syndrome': https://hbr.org/2021/02/stop-telling-women-they-have-imposter-syndrome, accessed 1 April 2023

Psychology Today gives a good overview of imposter syndrome here: https://www.psychologytoday.com/gb/basics/imposter-syndrome, accessed 1 April 2023

Samantha Boardman, '5 Ways to Overcome Imposter Syndrome': https://www.psychologytoday.com/gb/blog/positive-prescription/202303/5-ways-to-overcome-imposter-syndrome, accessed 1 April 2023

Chapter Six: The Journey in Search of Home and Belonging

John Clare, 'Home': https://interestingliterature.com/2019/02/home-a-poem-by-john-clare/, accessed 17 November 2023

Definition of *hiraeth*: https://www.bbc.com/travel/article/20210214-the-welsh-word-you-cant-translate, accessed 4 May 2023

D. C. D. Pocock, 'Place and the novelist', *Transactions of the Institute of British Geographers*, new series, vol. 6, no 3. (1981), p. 339

Marianna Pogosyan, 'The Sense that You Belong Somewhere': https://www.psychologytoday.com/gb/blog/between-cultures/202112/the-sense-you-belong-somewhere, accessed 6 May 2023

Kelly-Ann Allen, Margaret L. Kern, Christopher S. Rozek, Dennis M. McInerney and George M. Slavich, 'Belonging: a review of conceptual issues, an integrative framework, and directions for future research': https://www.tandfonline.com/doi/full/10.1080/00049530.2021.1883409, accessed 6 May 2023

For more about Socratic thinking and the exercise on reframing your thoughts: https://positivepsychology.com/cbt-cognitive-restructuring-cognitive-distortions/, accessed 7 May 2023

Part Four: Autumn in the Woods

Christina Rossetti, 'Autumn': https://poets.org/poem/autumn-9, accessed 17 November 2023

Chapter Seven: The Journey of Embracing Menopause

Charlotte Brontë, 'Life': https://www.poemhunter.com/poem/life/, accessed 13 December 2023

Statistics for how many people are affected by menopause, and whether or not men have an equivalent: https://www.engage. england.nhs.uk/safety-and-innovation/menopause-in-the-workplace/, accessed 14 May 2023

Quote from the Menopause Charity: https://www.themenopause charity.org/2021/10/21/the-effects-of-longterm-hormone-deficiency/, accessed 14 May 2023

Brianna M. Wright, Eva H. Stredulinsky, Graeme M. Ellis and John K.B. Ford, 'Kin-directed food sharing promotes lifetime natal philopatry of both sexes in a population of fish-eating killer whales, *Orcinus orca*': *Animal Behaviour*, vol. 115, May 2016, pp. 81–95; https://www.sciencedirect.com/science/article/pii/ S0003347216000737, accessed 14 May 2023

Dr Kirtly Parker Jones is interviewed about menopause on the University of Utah's website: https://healthcare.utah.edu/ the-scope/health-library/all/2016/11/new-treatment-womens-menopausal-symptoms, accessed 14 May 2023

The Balance App is available from Dr Louise Newson's fabulous website: https://www.balance-menopause.com/, accessed 14 May 2023

The NHS statistics for HRT treatment: https://media.nhsbsa.nhs.uk/ news/nhs-publishes-new-hrt-official-statistics, accessed 3 October 2023

The NICE guidelines for HRT as a treatment for hormone deficiency: https://www.nice.org.uk/guidance/ng23/chapter/ Recommendations#long-term-benefits-and-risks-of-hormone-replacement-therapy, accessed 14 May 2023

The information regarding archē, or 'principle', as an ancient Greek philosophical term comes from the *Routledge Encyclopaedia of Philosophy*: https://www.rep.routledge.com/articles/thematic/ arche/v-1, accessed 14 May 2023

The research carried out by Finestripe Productions and the Fawcett
Society: https://www.fawcettsociety.org.uk/menopauseandthe
workplace, accessed 14 May 2023

For information about early menopause or primary ovarian
insufficiency (POI): https://www.daisynetwork.org/, accessed
3 October 2023

Chapter Eight: The Journey Towards Reaching Your Potential – Self-Actualisation

Rūmi, 'You Were Born With Wings': https://www.goodreads.com/
quotes/439208-you-were-born-with-potential-you-were-born-
with-goodness, accessed 13 December 2023

Abraham Maslow, 'A Theory of Human Motivation' (1943):
https://psychclassics.yorku.ca/Maslow/motivation.htm, accessed
26 May 2023

Francesco Dimitri's book is called *That Sense of Wonder: How to
Capture the Miracles of Everyday Life* (Head of Zeus, 2018)

Actuation tests: https://positivepsychology.com/self-actualization-
tests-tools-maslow/, accessed 26 May 2023

Wild swimming website: http://www.wildswimming.co.uk/, accessed
1 March 2023

Sea and river pollution data: http://environment.data.gov.uk/bwq/
profiles/, accessed 16 October 2023

And also the Surfer's Against Sewage website (which has a handy
app) – https://www.sas.org.uk/water-quality/sewage-pollution-
alerts/ accessed 16 October 2023

The Manifesto of the Perfectly Imperfect Life

Rudyard Kipling, *op. cit.*

Alua Arthur's TED talk, 'Why Thinking about Death Helps You Live
a Better Life': https://www.youtube.com/watch?v=IkeuKPZxEhM,
accessed 5 July 2023